Polish Memories

Witold Gombrowicz

· · · · · · · · · · · · · · · · · ·

Polish Memories

Translated by Bill Johnston

Yale University Press / New Haven & London

Designed by Nancy Ovedovitz
Set in Minion type by Integrated Publishing Solutions.
Printed in the United States of America by R. R. Donnelly & Sons.

Library of Congress Cataloging-in-Publication Data
Gombrowicz, Witold.
[Wspomnienia polskie. English]
Polish memories / Witold Gombrowicz ; translated by Bill Johnston.
p.   cm.
ISBN 0-300-10410-3 (alk. paper)
1. Gombrowicz, Witold. 2. Authors, Polish—20th century—Biography.
I. Johnston, Bill. II. Title.
PG7158.G6692A38713 2004
891.8′5′37—dc22   2004014633

A catalogue record for this book is available from the British Library.

The paper in this book meets the guidelines for permanence and durability
of the Committee on Production Guidelines for Book Longevity
of the Council on Library Resources.

10   9   8   7   6   5   4   3   2   1

Polish Memories

"I was born and raised in a most respectable home": This ironic sentence, which begins one of my short stories–"The Memoirs of Stefan Czarniecki"—may also serve as an opening for these present recollections. I was indeed a milksop from a so-called "respectable" family, but here the word *respectable* should be used without irony, since it was a home of people who generally speaking were kind-hearted and had their principles.

My father owned a small property in Sandomierz province and also worked in industry; when I was growing up he was president of Central Salvage and a member of several supervisory committees and governing boards, which guaranteed him an income considerably greater than that produced by tiny Małoszyce. My mother was the daughter of Ignacy Kotkowski, a local landowner. My father was originally from Lithuania; my grandfather, Onufry, had had his property confiscated by the Russian government in 1863, and this led him to move to the Kingdom, where with the little money he had managed to hold on to he bought the village of Jakubowice, and then a second, Małoszyce, where I was born.

We Gombrowiczes always regarded ourselves as "rather better" than the landed gentry of the Sandomierz region, particularly because of various family connections that had remained from the times in Lithuania, and also because the Lithuanian gentry, richer and settled for centuries on their possessions, could boast of a better tradition, a more detailed history, and more respectable appointments. I'm not convinced, though, that the Sandomierz gentry shared this point of view. I was the youngest child. Janusz was the oldest, then came Jerzy, and then my sister, Irena, who was two years older than I was.

My life in Poland was uneventful and unchanging; I knew few exceptional people and had few adventures. But I'd like to show, though I do not know whether it will be of use to anyone, the way in which life shaped me—me and my literature. Naturally this will be very much an incomplete testimony, which will often remain on the surface of events, because this is not the place for more exhausting analyses or more ruthless confessions; yet I believe that even this toned-down biography will shed a small ray of light on the realities of Poland in those days. It would also be good if at the same time I were able to convey how today I regard the Poland of that time— from a perspective of twenty years spent abroad, a western, American perspective.

In Poland I think that only a few people know me from an extensive reading of my books, which are admittedly somewhat difficult and eccentric. There are more who have heard of me; for them I am above all the author of the "mug" and the "bum"; it's through these two powerful myths that I have entered Polish letters. But what does it mean to "give someone a mug" or to "fix a bum on him"? To "give someone a mug" is to lend someone a different face than his own, to distort him. For instance, when I treat a wise person as a fool or impute criminal intentions to a good person, I give them a mug. And "fixing a bum on someone" is in fact an identical operation, the only difference being that in this case an adult is treated like a child, infantilized. As you can see, both these metaphors are connected with an act of deformation that one person commits upon another. And if I have occupied a separate place in our literature, it is perhaps above all because I've highlighted the extraordinary significance of form in both social and personal life. "One person creates the other"—this was my psychological starting point. I believe, too, that my sensitivity to form from earliest childhood allowed me later to find my own literary style and to create a genre that today is slowly acquiring adherents around the world.

Yet where did I get it, this sensitivity to human form—in other words, to a person's way of being? Once, before the war, in a lecture on my novel *Ferdydurke* the brilliant Polish artist Bruno Schulz said that this book was not made up, that it must have been the product of many difficult personal experiences. Schulz was not mistaken. In my own way I suffered considerably in the very early days of my existence; we shall speak at first of those torments of the Polish process of coming into being, in order later on to touch on other topics.

I shall begin from the fact that, appearances to the contrary, my family home was one immense dissonance constantly rending my child's ears. There were many reasons for this state of affairs; one of the most important was the incompatibility in temperament and character between my mother and my father.

My father, a handsome, dapper man—a "thoroughbred" as people would emphasize in those days—was considered serious, responsible, and honest. The contrast between his proper and dignified behavior and certain eccentricities manifested by us, his sons, produced many a reaction along the lines of "what would your father have to say about that," or "what a pity they didn't take after old Gombrowicz." His impeccable appearance, in combination with a mind that was neither particularly profound nor had especially wide horizons, yet which worked efficiently, secured for my father those mostly symbolic positions on various committees and boards.

My mother, on the other hand, was distinguished by an uncommonly lively nature and a fertile imagination. She was nervous, extravagant, inconsistent; she had no self-control. She was naive and, worst of all, had the most mistaken image of herself. Father often succumbed to her quick-wittedness and intelligence, but more often endured in silence her various exaltations, which were indeed hard to handle.

I don't wish to dwell overlong on my closest family. I will say that, in my view, it was my mother who introduced into our home the profound formal ambiguity within which I grew up. I don't blame her for this, since she had a noble character and the best of intentions, and she was exceedingly fond of us; but, despite her excellent command of French, various kinds of knowledge that constituted the education of a young lady of the gentry, and firm moral principles, she lacked that which gives an ordinary milking-girl such self-confidence, naturalness, and straightforwardness—she hadn't been tested by life. She had never really come into contact with it. This was what deprived her of authority in our eyes and meant that she moved about in a vacuum.

In this vacuum she no longer really knew who she was, and instead constructed for herself a personality that was sheer fantasy. "How much work I've put into this garden!" she would say as she showed visitors around the garden at Małoszyce, whereas we knew it was all the work of the gardener. "I confess it's a little strange, but I have a soft spot for philosophy and exact thinking; I love to read Spencer," she would say in the best faith, while we knew full well that the pages of the Spencer volumes had never even been cut open. "I've worked so hard bringing up the children"—but we were aware that the main burden of that work had fallen on the governess.

Thus, she saw herself as a "woman of hard work and principles," "fulfilling her obligations," "systematic, exact, with a gift for management and organization," whereas in reality she was the opposite of all this—fanciful, feckless, incapable of systematic effort, and accustomed to the various privileges that money provides. I do not in the least hold it against my mother that she was the way she was. She also had many good qualities, though of a different sort—goodness, nobility, integrity, intelligence—and her weaknesses were partly a consequence of her nerves, and partly the result of her artificial life and no less artificial upbringing.

But the fact that she did not wish to be what she was, to confess to her true self, took its revenge on her, for we, her sons, declared war on her. She infuriated us. And I believe it was from this that there began my painful adventures with the various distortions of Polish form, which acted on me like tickling: A person laughs to bursting, but it is not a pleasant sensation.

*

The war that my older brothers and I waged on my mother primarily involved a systematic refutation of anything she said. It was enough that my mother should casually mention it was raining, for an overwhelming force to impel me immediately to declare with studied astonishment, as if I had just heard the most absurd thing: "What do you mean! The sun's shining brightly!"

I think this early training in evident falsehood and open preposterousness proved immensely useful in later years when I began to write.

But, bearing in mind that there were three of us—my sister took no part in this game—our home gradually began to resemble a lunatic asylum, and it was only my father's strictness and gravity that saved us from utter catastrophe. The constant, insane polemics with my mother extended to every possible sphere—the philosophical, the moral, the religious, the societal, the familial, and the social. If mother praised someone we would have to condemn that person. If she liked something, we would not rest till we had identified its faults. Her extraordinary naivety meant that on every occasion she would allow herself to be dragged anew into these bizarre discussions—which, of course, amused us even more. What fun it was! Those games permitted us to forget deeper and more dramatic irritations that lay hidden beneath the surface, and made it easier to deal with our mother. It was probably from here that there emerged in my later work the cult of play and an understanding of its colossal significance in culture.

This particular game was led by my brother Jerzy, a born comic and jokester with an artistic nature who was gifted with a considerable sense of the dramatic and a huge inventiveness when it came to various sayings, some of which I continue to plagiarize flagrantly today. At that time I was thoroughly under his influence. The polemics with our mother also required the broaching of especially controversial subjects with the aim of provoking discussion; the topic of divorce was particularly well suited to this, since mother was a devout Catholic and a person of what were known as "principles."

"Another divorce in the family!" Jerzy would announce loudly from the front door, to which I would respond from the other end of the house: "What?! Another divorce in the family? Surely not!"

"Just imagine," Jerzy would shout across four rooms, "in the tram I met Aunt Róża, who swore to me that Ela's divorcing her third husband!"

"I don't believe it!" I would call out with great pathos, in order to lure mother from her bedroom. And a debate would ensue in which we would maintain the thesis that divorces are an excellent invention, since "the children acquire a double set of parents" and "are overjoyed to have two homes to choose from instead of one."

I also remember a discussion about whether one of our cousins was right to play bridge with her three ex-husbands. We asserted that this was a sign of great breeding.

As you can see, it was fine training in dialectics, and was greatly admired by our maid Aniela: "You should hear the way the young masters carry on with Mrs. Gombrowicz!" Of course, I won't defend the views we espoused, but such mockery of perhaps over-stiff principles is not an entirely unhealthy thing. My mother had a social life; for some time she was president of the Society of Landed Ladies, a most pious institution marked by an incurably high-flown style. We, naturally with wild glee, would bring those flights to earth, and I even listened in on meetings from behind the door so as to garner material for our satires. But all this was not merely a game. Deep down, we were ever more prey to the suspicion that we ourselves were also affected by the sickness of "unreality" that we fought with in our mother; for we were beginning to sense, if not to understand, that, like her, we had not been tested by life and had never properly come into contact with it.

I'm touching here on one of my most painful sore points, which exerted a major influence on my development. And I have no doubt that the same sickness infected the whole of the so-called upper classes in Poland, with the exception only of hardworking professionals such as physicians or engineers whose everyday labors rubbed up against reality. But the landed gentry, and the wealthy bourgeoisie, and the greater part of the intelligentsia—these were people who led privileged lives and who were unfamiliar with any real struggle either for existence or for its values. How typical it was that my father, for example, only very rarely and as it were by chance became conscious of the abnormal nature of his social situation, whereas we, the next generation, saw everything much more sharply and clearly. For my father, a valet was the most natural of things and required no explanation; and even when later on, as we became more democratic, we took a maid instead of a valet, he still allowed himself to be waited on as if it belonged to the innate order of the world. My father was a master in a natural way, in all unconstraint, and I must admit that simple people instinctively responded to his naturalness and were much more willing to busy themselves around him than around us—shrunken masters who tried to compensate with the faces they made.

My mother also treated being a lady as the most natural thing in the world. My parents belonged to a generation that had never, in a social sense, experienced what Hegel termed "bad consciousness." They believed that people should live at the level where fate has placed them, fulfilling the obligations that fall to them because they belong to a particular sphere. Masters should be good masters, and servants good servants—that was their entire philosophy. Anything else was a pipe dream thought up by theorists.

For us, however, the younger generation, these things soon began to make themselves felt. But in that early youth of mine—when I was roughly between fourteen and eighteen years of age—I was not so sensitive to the moral aspects of the matter, and more aware of the personal humiliations associated with this inequality. As long as I was in Warsaw everything was more or less bearable. But when I went to the country on vacation, the drama would begin.

I was friends with various boys my age, the sons of farmers and grooms. This had come about because when I was still a little kid of ten, Janusz had organized for me a "guard," that is, a company of village boys whom I commanded. Of course, even then I went through great torments, because during drills my mother or the governess would call from a distance that I shouldn't get my feet wet or ask "Aren't you cold in that?" In helpless, mute, agonized rage, I received this feminine disgrace that was so cynical, so oblivious to the harm being done to me. My situation was most unusual. In theory I was the leader, the young master, a higher being born to command. In practice, all the attributes of my superiority—my shoes, my scarf, my governess, and, horror of horrors, my galoshes—thrust me into the depths of mortification; and it was with a surreptitious, carefully concealed admiration that I regarded the bare feet and coarse shirts of my subordinates. That exceptionally strong impression remained with me permanently, and in later years it found expression in my art, in the form of satire on the subject of lordliness, superiority, and maturity.

Thus, at about the age of ten, I had discovered something awful: that we "masters" were an utterly grotesque and ludicrous phenomenon, something foolish, painfully comic, and even abhorrent. Yes indeed! I cared little whether we were exploiters of the common people or about our morality, but I was appalled that we look so absurd in comparison to ordinary people. It was America that finally cured me of this complex.

*

When I was eleven years old—this was in 1915—a big change took place in my life: My parents sent me to school. This establishment, the Stanisław Kostka Philological Grammar School, was at the time located rather shabbily on some floor of some courtyard in a building on Bracka Street, though it was soon to move to more commodious premises at the corner of Traugutta and Krakowskie Przedmieście.

I was terrified. It was a matter not just of my sensitivity, but also my rustic timidity, my lack of experience with people that was so typical of the sons of the gentry. And the first years were in fact painful. I entered the second grade, and so I was one of the youngest; and because I had a restless and contrary temperament, I soon became the victim of every possible variety of corkscrew, single and double scissors, nelsons, and garden-variety kicks and punches. I recall in particular two forms of torture. One involved passing the back of the hand over the victim's hair, which in some diabolic way made it feel like it was being torn out by the roots; the other didn't hurt so much yet was also harder to avoid—it involved kicks delivered "flat, from the side."

I immediately fell amongst a group of fearful bullies who became my tormenters. And every morning as I set off for school with my neatly packed satchel, I knew that before I managed to unpack it Braksal would descend upon me and give me a drilling, while Wasiński would "do my hair."

Despite this I didn't relegate myself to the ranks of the milksops, but instead set about finding allies and organizing an aggressive-defensive bloc; this was made easier the following year when I was joined in the school by Kazio Baliński, my good friend, the son of Ignacy Baliński the senator and chairman of the City Council, and younger brother of the poet Stanisław. Kazio and Zaza Baliński, Antoś Wasiutyński, and I had previously had private lessons together with Mrs. Kiersnowska. And so when Kazio, Antoś, and I found ourselves in the same school we immediately formed a pact, which was later joined by Tadzio Kępiński, a close friend of Baliński's. But before this came about, before I settled in somewhat in that house of tears and learned its little ways, I experienced great sufferings, to the accompaniment of the perpetrators' fearful snickering.

In those first years I dreamed of being older and entering the senior classes, which seemed a heavenly oasis of civilization compared to my present hell with its clamor, its rushing about, its attacks and evasions, its constant state of ferment, without a moment's peace—and on top of it all the filth and ugliness of those face-pulling whelps. *L'âge ingrat*—the ungracious age—is what it's called in French. One of the most curious discoveries I made in my subsequent travels to the West was that this ungracious age manifested itself in Germany, or in Italy for instance, much less forcefully; boys there were so much less monstrous. And when I found myself in Argentina it turned out that here there is virtually no ungracious age at all. The elegance, poise, and properness of an Argentinian child of that age is truly enviable.

If I were to visit Poland for a few months, as I intended to just last year, first and foremost I would take a look at the children to determine whether there has been an improvement since the times of my childhood; for me, this would give a better measure of the progress of Polish culture than the entire literary and scientific output of the last forty years. Naturally it shouldn't be assumed that, in my disgust at my grotesque chums, I myself was some sort of little junior Petronius, unfamiliar with pimples, dirty ears, and dirty fingernails. Rather the opposite—along with such problems, I was additionally prey to various others. These were mostly poses, mannerisms, pretending to be blasé or acting the smart aleck, adopting a pretentious estheticism— in a word, the fruit of an excess of imagination and, to some extent, of the atmosphere of my home. Today it's easy for me to speak of these things, but at the time it was truly terrible and I truly did suffer— surrounded by frenetic hideousness, while I myself was no better!

The Stanisław Kostka Grammar School was exceedingly aristo-cratic. It was crammed with Radziwiłłs, Potockis, Tyszkiewiczes, and Platers. But there was also no shortage of boys from lesser social classes. The superior appearance of these "blue bloods," as my friend Adamski used to call them, and a certain elegance they possessed, immediately drew my attention. Even amongst us young pups they stood out as more European, and they were not devoid of refine-ment. In general the aristocracy kept to itself and admitted to its ranks only a small number of fortunates, some of whom were related to them, but all from families that belonged to so-called society. This took place with a precision striking in ones so young, by a kind of natural selection, and probably unconsciously. Yet the inflexible and uncompromising quality of that aristocratic taboo in the context of our unrestrained, clamorous anarchy became for me the manifesta-tion of an unwritten law—one of those that, the less they are trum-peted, the more they make themselves felt. Kazio Baliński's grand-mother was a countess (though not one of the first rank), while his great-grandmother had been a duchess and of course his father was a senator; he was one of the chosen ones who might conceivably be admitted. I had several aunts who were countesses, and at a pinch I too could have mingled with the likes of Bisio Tyszkiewicz or Władek Potocki and accompanied them on our way home from school. But neither Kazio nor I made any effort in this direction. By that time I think I had already acquired the inability—which caused me so much harm in later life—to associate with those of higher station than myself. This wasn't because of an inferiority complex; rather, it arose from the fact that I already had my own special way of being, and I only felt comfortable with those on whom I could impose this form. The aristocracy, on the other hand, had its own genre, which was so clearly defined, and at the same time so banal and impersonal, that I would have been helpless and would have had to toe the line.

Let me remind you of my previous confession—do you remem-ber?—regarding the village boys, that personal guard of mine, whom

I commanded, secretly admiring them for the fact that they went barefoot and didn't wear overshoes. By then already I could see two kinds of beauty which were available to me, that is, which were relevant to my boyish years. One was the simple, barefoot kind; the other, that of those boys from the best families in the country, unquestionable thoroughbreds gifted from the very dawn of their existence with elegance and even distinction, and forming a closed clan. Which should be chosen? It wasn't an easy matter, since when all was said and done my nature, the nature of an artist, deep down was instinctively aristocratic—don't forget that an artist has an instinctual feeling for hierarchy, superiority, and refinement, and that art consists of the ruthless segregation of values, the selection of that which is higher and better, and a scornful rejection of that which is common and of indifferent quality.

It would have been no surprise, then, had I chosen the Potockis and the Radziwiłłs, just as they had been chosen by Chopin, or Proust, or Balzac. Yet on the other hand, even then I'd noticed certain small but disgusting things—yes, disgusting—in that aristocracy, which, when I was fourteen years of age, gave me pause for thought.

For example, nose picking. Yes, nose picking. I observed that the aristocracy gladly engaged in this pursuit. I also observed that the nose picking of my village boys was somehow innocent and inoffensive, while the same operation carried out by the hand of a Potocki or a Wielopolski became something terribly unpleasant and repulsive.

This powerful discovery began to lead me toward the left. But at the same time a wave of snobbery overcame me and for a long time interrupted my development.

*

In those years the world war awakened in me an incurable longing for the West.

I mention this because I believe it is a very Polish sentiment, and one that is as alive today as it was then. One of my mother's closest friends was Mrs. Mikułowska-Pomorska, whose husband, a professor, was a supporter of the Central Powers and served as a minister in the government of the Regency Council. Under their influence, my mother also began to manifest somewhat pro-German sympathies, which of course was all that was needed for us, my brothers and me, to declare ourselves passionately on the side of the Entente.

I pored over the news from the front, took a pencil, and, with a solemn mien, marked on the map every little village around Rheims or Amiens that was taken, as if the entire war depended on it. For me, Europe began on the other side of that front; the Russians and Germans were a second-rate existence, laughable, barbaric, separating us from the other place—from civilization. I sensed, I knew, that over there was my world, my homeland, my destiny. When in 1918 the dam cracked and the West began to leak, just seeping through to begin with, this for me was as important as the regaining of independence. I was in the crowd that greeted Paderewski; I ate "western" chocolate brought by Janek Baliński's American friends; I gazed at the uniforms of Haller's soldiers; from a distance I saw the car from the French embassy.

At that time, in the country at Małoszyce I had the following conversation with my older brother:

"It'd be good to have some kind of walkway built to avoid having to wade in mud when you go to the barn or the stables."

"It'd be a waste of time!"

"Why?"

"Because mud is mud! If I have a walkway made, in three days they'll smash it up. But you can't smash mud up. Mud is mud!"

"Mud is mud here! Not in other countries! Other countries know how to deal with it. It's only here that mud is the kind of mud that'll always be mud."

"You're daft! Those are daydreams! You have to think realistically. Conditions are different here."

Conditions are different! For me, Europe was above all those *other conditions*. There, things were not dominated by that awful realism which is typical for the whole of the East and which I had heard at such length from various uncles and what have you, a realism that is fearfully submissive toward nature and is filled with the conviction that filth really *is* inevitable and that one has no choice but to wallow in it. I imagined France and England precisely as if over there, one emerged from the mud and found firm ground under one's feet, and one's confidence and freedom of movement returned.

Later on, in America I encountered the same oppressive longing for Europe. People who knew they could never afford to cross the Atlantic would buy something European—some porcelain, a map of Paris or Rome—and preserve it like a sacred object. I even knew some who thanks to those maps were more conversant with the topography of Paris than a native Parisian.

How splendid was that year of 1918! I was still too young to appreciate the entire beauty of the First World War's finale, so very much more instinct with poetry than the ending of the Second World War. It was a kind of emotional awakening to a new life filled with promise, an obliteration of monarchs' thrones and stiff collars, moustaches and mistaken beliefs about "honor," freedom of the body mixing with freedom of spirit, the rout of frock coats and patent-leather shoes, a great relaxation of young people welcoming their era, a great wind of liberty as women's knees appeared from under their skirts. I wasn't intoxicated by this, unlike the poets of the Picador group, later to become the Skamander movement, who were a few years older than I; but I did sense the electricity in the air of Europe! That word excited me no less than the word *Poland*. Europe, bloodied but already shining, rising like a moon over what had been the Russian's "land on the Vistula," their Polish province.

I didn't formulate this clearly, but I felt that in the distance there had appeared some kind of chance to free myself from the ugliness of Poland that oppressed me so.

In those days I would spend my afternoons at the Balińskis, whose home was, as the expression went, "enlightened," "cultured," rich in contacts with Paris and London, and no stranger to literature and art. Of course, I had no access to the formal breakfasts at which chairman Ignacy received the papal nuncio and other members of the diplomatic corps, but from time to time Staś Baliński would see fit to initiate us youngsters, Kazio, Zaza, and me, into the doings of the Picador and Skamander poets, who were beginning their poetic offensive. This was my first encounter with literature. I attended in wonder to that solemn gossip concerning the various follies, eccentricities, and provocations of Tuwim, Lechoń, and Słonimski, and I was all ears as I listened to their early poems, understanding virtually nothing. Through all this I remained provincial to the core, a timid bumpkin, a bit of a milksop; and though in my mind the awakening novelty of Polish life was an intense experience, in practice I was unable to enter into contact with it.

I doubt whether it ever occurred to Staś that the timid and callow Ita (this nickname had been brought back from Japan by my godfather, General Dowbór-Muśnicki, and it was how I was known at the time), that Ita would one day be transformed into enemy number one of the Skamander movement and of many other things that he, Staś, held in esteem—he had no idea he was nourishing a viper in his bosom. It must still be difficult for him today to believe that the Gombrowicz of *Ferdydurke* and the *Diary* is the same meek Ita from years ago who listened religiously to his poetic revelations.

Because at that time I was incapable of expressing myself! To almost anyone! With older people, with my parents, with relatives, and with strangers it was as if I were paralyzed; it was only with a few of my closest companions that I regained a (rather impressive) ability to speak. And within me a rebelliousness was growing that I could neither comprehend nor control. I remember the funeral of a relative in which I took part. The Balińskis were walking behind the casket, very properly, along with many other people. All at once I was taken over by some demon, and I began to behave provocatively: I stuck my hands in my pockets, kicked at whatever was lying on the road, ogled the women, and then, to my parents' dismay, I began chatting loudly with other equally disconcerted mourners. Then finally, when we reached the cemetery, I was overcome by uncontrollable laughter, and as I stood at the graveside I was choking from helpless giggling.

Another time I went to talk to our art teacher, who was a painter; I don't recall his name.

"I went to your exhibition, sir," I said out of the blue, "but I really didn't like the pictures. They're useless! It was a real embarrassment! I'm surprised at you, sir!"

This painter had an advantage over me that painters of the present day do not. He grabbed me by the ear and stood me against the wall in the school office, where for a whole hour I swallowed tears of indignation and humiliation.

The older I grew, the more dangerous I became. My work in Polish class was best, and that saved me, because in other subjects I was a dunce and a loafer. One day Mr. Ciepliński, our Polish teacher, assigned us an essay on Słowacki. I was tired of the endless adulation of the bard, and I decided to let him have it for a change. The opening, to the best of my recollection, ran as follows: "Juliusz Słowacki, the thief who stole from Byron and Shakespeare and was incapable of inventing anything of his own." The rest was by no means inferior to the introduction. Mr. Ciepliński gave me an F and threatened to send my essay to the ministry, upon which I asked him why he forced his students into hypocrisy. And in order to destroy him, in front of the whole class I recited a passage from his, Ciepliński's, volume of poetry: "Moonlight pours upon the pines and slender firs."

*

I was sixteen and had graduated from the sixth grade when the dramatic summer of 1920 came along. That vacation I spent in the country, at Małoszyce. The war reports were becoming ever more alarming, and in the end began to reach even my youthful consciousness. The Bolsheviks were drawing closer. One day, I don't remember for what reason, we returned to Warsaw and there I lived through the decisive days of August.

This was a tough experience. I had few memories of the world war, since I was still a child. It was only now that I felt war, war with the additional fear of revolution, and with something even more painful for me—fear of military service.

At that time, all the young people were volunteering; almost all of my friends were in uniform by then, while the city was plastered with posters bearing a pointing finger and a slogan saying something along the lines of "The fatherland is calling you." Young women would ask young men on the street, "Why aren't you in the army yet?" I remember my grandmother was appalled at this. "Can you imagine, Tosia," she would say to my mother, "what times these must be, how brazen these girls are, accosting young men like that without a second thought? I mean, a young fellow could simply reply: 'You're not to my liking, miss!'" But soon even grandmother stopped worrying about what was proper and what wasn't; things were starting to heat up.

For me the army was a specter. Not war, not battles, but precisely the barracks, the uniforms, the sergeant, the drills—the whole military way of life, which to me was hateful and unthinkable. At the age of sixteen, I had often thought anxiously about the military service that awaited me in five years' time; and here a practical joke played by history meant that girls on the street were already harassing me with "And why are you not in uniform, young man?" True, I was the youngest in my class; but I myself understood that this was merely an excuse. True, my mother, who was horrified, condemned the government for "recruiting children"; but I was fully aware that this was an expression of her existential fear for her own child. In one respect at least I was up to the situation: I didn't deceive myself and did not conceal from myself the fact that I was afraid of the army and that I was useless.

How humiliating it was! The more so because I suffered from no illness or disability; on the surface it looked as though there were nothing wrong with me. Then was I a coward? Today, I can look upon that cowardice of mine more calmly; I know that my nature was calling me to certain particular tasks and was developing in me other qualities that had nothing in common with the army. But a boy of sixteen doesn't yet know anything of himself, and there is no salvation for him if he's not like all the other boys of his age. That year of 1920 turned me into a creature "unlike all the others," apart, living on the margins of society. I live such a marginal life to this day; later in my recollections I'll perhaps try to explain how this kind of isolation from society can be reconciled with work like literature that is social in its essence. This break with the crowd, with the nation, forcing me to seek my own paths and to live by my own efforts, began for me in that memorable year of the Battle of Warsaw.

My mother's firm opposition overcame the will of my father, who tried to demand that I "do my duty." I was assigned to some civilian institution—I don't remember what it was called—whose mission was to send packages to the soldiers at the front. It was located in the main university building and employed a number of young ladies as well as a number of boys whose parents, like mine, had "not allowed them to join the army."

I would find it hard to describe my frame of mind at that time, crucial as it was for my entire future development. I was mortified, and at the same time I was in a state of rebellion; these experiences drove me to anarchy and cynicism, and for the first time I turned against the fatherland, the state, and other instruments of collective pressure on the individual. I had enough integrity not to use empty phrases to joke my way out of a situation whose unequivocal character was unquestionable. I had no right to be a patriot, since I had avoided military service at such a moment. True, I was not the only one whose parents had not permitted him to join the army; there were many sixteen-year-olds in various civilian institutions. But this sort of argument was humbug, and I preferred to face up to the truth. At the time, however, I wasn't capable of opposing the crowd with a philosophy in defense of the individual; I could only respond with rebelliousness. I had the feeling that I was alone, alone against everyone, and that I needed to close in on myself and forbid access to anyone else.

The fact that a young man is sent to the army by force; that he's made to swear an oath, and that this coerced oath is treated as a voluntary commitment; that he remains for one or two years the slave of the sergeants and officers; that he is required to show blind obedience and to sacrifice his own life—all this may be acceptable only to those who already have their military service behind them, or to those for whom routine and custom have taken the place of a direct experience of reality.

My cousin, Bebuś Rosset, would visit us from time to time. He was an officer in the 1st Uhlan Regiment, which was famed for its exploits, and he brought with him the atmosphere of the front and the battle. Once I asked him, "How can you put your own life at risk just because some other fellow tells you to?"

"The person who tells me to," Bebuś answered in his eastern lilt, "isn't some fellow, but a superior officer, an authority."

"What authority?" I replied. "If he took his clothes off he'd be the same as you, or worse. So why should he be able to send you to your death?"

He didn't explain it to me, but started singing:

> See: From the barrel of a gun
> Death stares out at everyone
> I may survive the war
> And see my Lwów once more
> The town that I adore.

In general that was how people responded to me. With songs, or jokes, or—in the best case—trite arguments on the topic of duty and so on. I was still a hundred miles from an intellectual grasp of these difficult issues, but I was already beginning to understand that human life in Poland is cheap. In western literature, above all that in French, which I had begun to study, the individual is assigned more value. There, a person and that person's existence are a serious matter, perhaps more important than the fates of states and nations. I also tried to understand something of Kant's *Prolegomena to All Future Metaphysics*, and here too I was shown the fundamental significance of the "I" that was so slighted in my native country.

I believe that that year of 1920 made me what I have remained to the present day—an individualist. And this came about because I was not able to fulfill my obligations toward the nation at a time of imminent threat to our freshly minted independence. This put me in a situation of coercion—I had no choice. Patriotism without a willingness to sacrifice one's life for the fatherland was for me an empty word. Because that willingness was not in me, I had to accept the consequences.

Of course, in my later development all these agitations of youth settled down and became more civilized. But they did not go away. Recently a certain eminent scholar and recipient of the Nobel Prize read one of my books and expressed surprise that I was not very Polish—because for him, Poles meant heroic deaths on the battlefield, Chopin, uprisings, and the ruins of Warsaw. I replied: "I am a Pole brought to extremities by History."

*

The fall of that year—1920—I spent in Małoszyce. The high schools were closed, since almost all the upperclassmen were still serving as volunteers in the army. Thus, after the fiercest days of the defense of Warsaw and Piłsudski's victorious offensive, I was sent to the country to make up for a summer wasted in the city.

Those few months in Małoszyce are inscribed in my memory as particularly disagreeable. You already know how demoralized I was by the fact that I hadn't signed up like the rest of my friends. I returned to Małoszyce in a state of humiliation and at the same time of rebellion. There was no one there except for the staff and Mrs. Bednarczyk, the housekeeper, with whom I played chess. It was strange: One would think that the whole welter of feelings and thoughts that had been stirred up by the war crisis and my personal loss of face would lead me to some sort of painful inner conflict; yet in fact, it found release in an attack of pathological snobbishness!

My older brother Jerzy had for some time been working on our family archive, several hundred documents that dated back to the end of the fifteenth century. He took them out of a chest, organized them, and began to study the Gombrowicz family's past. At the time I copied him closely, so I also adopted this obsession, and soon I had acquired a rather extensive knowledge of these documents. The first literary work of my life was a monograph I wrote in those years of the *illustrissimae familiae Gombrovici,* as I pretentiously christened it. It remained in typescript. Actually it contained nothing of particular interest, since the Gombrowiczes had never risen beyond the gentry; but every detail concerning their possessions, the offices they held, or their connections filled me with pleasure and caused me to put on ever greater airs.

How can this foolish snobbery be reconciled with my other qualities, which had made me a shrewd and critical boy with a strong sense of the comic? How did it relate to my anarchy, my rebelliousness, my philosophical readings, my fondness for modernity? It's a mystery. At one and the same time I was wise beyond my years and terrifyingly callow, cynical and naive, European and provincial, modern and old-fashioned; all this was inside of me, producing jarring dissonances, playacting, falseness, and embarrassment!

Even today I blush with shame as I recall those painful gaucheries from forty years ago.

Here's one of them. At the culminating moment of the fighting on the outskirts of Warsaw, in the office where I worked as a volunteer sending out packages, as if by the by I showed my boss a photograph of an imposing building.

"This is the palace of my cousin, Mrs. Tyszkiewicz, at Wistycz," I mentioned, also by the by.

"That building's in Lublin," my boss replied drily as he stared at the photograph, and he even named the institution that it housed. "I know it like the back of my hand," he added.

I encountered such reverses all the time. I became artificial, affected. My aunts would comment regretfully: "That poor Itek! He's become so blasé! He poses so!" My artificiality brought out artificiality in the people with whom I came into contact. I was unhappy. I couldn't find my place in the world. Everything I did came out badly, awkwardly; everything made me ridiculous and inadequate.

It was in a dour mood, then, that I left for Małoszyce. The days were autumnal, melancholy, and lonely. I sometimes went hunting for hares, but mostly just rambled about the countryside. I tried to impress Mrs. Bednarczyk with my pitiful genealogy.

One day, I no longer remember why, a group of officers who were friends of Jerzy's came to Małoszyce. I forgot to serve them vodka during dinner—them, cavalry officers—this was the extent of my stupefaction! I was so indifferent to everything that I gave them the vodka after the meal. I wandered the fields with my head hung low, and squashed clods of earth with the tip of my boot.

The world became impossible for me. Everything was like a malicious caricature. My family and my social "sphere" were overbearing, pampered, soft. Society, the nation, the state were my enemies. The army was a bad dream. Ideals and ideologies were empty phrases. And I myself was the worst, the most artificial and pretentious one of all. Every word I uttered came out wrong, and every gesture was contaminated.

God had somehow disappeared from view: It wasn't exactly that I had ceased to believe, so much as that faith no longer interested me—I had stopped thinking about it. Because of this, my isolation was rendered complete. At the same time, as I maundered about the countryside, I would gaze at my companions of earlier years, the village boys of my former "guard," who now were already working. They weren't caricatures! They were plain and straightforward—genuine somehow. Each word of theirs sounded right. I couldn't comprehend how culture, education, and upbringing can render a person false, while illiteracy produces such positive results. Until finally, a certain thought occurred to me. This revelation came upon me on my way back to Warsaw, in strange and dramatic circumstances.

I boarded the train at Ćmielów, and at the next stop, Bodzechów, an elderly uncle of mine, a landowner of the Sandomierz province, also got on. He too was traveling to Warsaw, and he took a seat next to me in a first-class compartment, which was packed: In those days one sat anywhere, without paying any attention which carriage it was. My uncle was an excellent marksman and we talked about hunting, though I didn't know the first thing on the subject. All of a sudden, my uncle looked around the compartment and said in a quiet but clear voice, "Please leave."

Our fellow travelers looked at him in surprise. Then my uncle reached into his pocket, took out a revolver, released the safety catch, and repeated without raising his voice, "Please leave."

This time the compartment emptied in the blink of an eye. A hullabaloo arose in the corridor; the conductor was called, and women were crying. My uncle locked the door of the compartment and said with a roguish wink: "At last we have a bit of room. There was such a crowd I could hardly hear myself think. My nerves aren't so good; I've not been sleeping well. I'm going to Warsaw to try and improve the situation, because if it gets worse, so will everything else."

I realized that he had gone mad. He'd gone mad and would start shooting if provoked. I was drenched with perspiration. I managed to explain to the conductor that my uncle shouldn't be excited and that I would try and ensure that he reached Warsaw. The rest of the journey, which took several hours, I spent alone with a madman who didn't part with his revolver even for a second. I had to entertain him with conversation, and in the end, not knowing what tack to take,

I tried appealing to his ambition: "It's a terrible thing," I said, "that every landowner has to be an eccentric and behave as if he had bats in his belfry."

"You think so?" said my uncle. "You really find the gentry so eccentric? It's true, by God—I've often noticed the same thing myself. They're all so queer it's embarrassing. Have their estates gone to their heads or what?"

"You know, Uncle, I have a theory of my own," I replied hurriedly, to keep the conversation going. "Listen to this, it's rather interesting. You see, according to me, simple people have an advantage over us in that they lead a natural life. They have elementary needs, and as a result their values too are simple, unaffected, genuine. For example: A simple person is hungry, and so a value for him is bread."

"You don't say," declared my uncle politely.

"But for a wealthy person bread is no longer a value, because he has it in abundance. We live a privileged, artificial life. We have no need to struggle for our existence, and so we create artificial needs for ourselves. Then our values become cigarettes, or fashion, or genealogy, or hounds. This artificiality of needs produces an artificiality of form. That's why we're so eccentric and why it's so hard for us to find the right tone."

When, ten or fifteen years later, I recounted at a writers' table in the Ziemiańska café how it was thanks to fear of a loaded revolver that I independently struck upon what Marxists would call the dialectic of needs and values, I was shouted down and told I was making it up. Yet it really happened this way! And the notion of the artificiality of form amongst the upper classes was to become one of the starting points for my work as a writer.

*

After the upheaval of the war, school began with a delay of several months and without much enthusiasm, since the lanky youths who had gotten a taste of gunpowder had no desire for routine and rancid lessons in the wretched "jug." I felt the same way. True, Wasiński and Braksal had stopped "turning the screws" on me, and my intellectual ascendancy assured me a minimal respect in the seventh grade; yet on the other hand, the absurdity of the curriculum and the entire method of teaching was manifested ever more clearly. In *Ferdydurke* you'll find an account of a Polish lesson and a Latin lesson, and a description of the "pedagogical body"; those scenes, filled with craziness, were already being born in my brain at that time, in the seventh grade, as I drowned in the mawkish lectures of Mr. Ciepliński, a decent enough person in his way, about the national bards of Poland, or as I stared in dismay at the grotesque, comical figure of our Latin teacher.

Here in Argentina, I've often meant to question visitors from Poland in detail about the present high school curriculum, but the conversation always turns to other, more pressing matters. I suspect that little has changed, since teaching is a fearfully ponderous and cumbersome apparatus abounding in fossilized people and fossilized ideas, in which the poor young pup who is the victim of education is really in the back of everyone's mind, and the most important thing is to employ the teachers, the thousands-strong legions of this bureaucracy. Furthermore, the school must still educate people "in the national spirit," and this entails an utterly distorted perspective on all of world culture. Local battles swell to the rank of epochal events, while truly significant facts are barely mentioned.

One day I had the following discussion with our Polish teacher, Mr. Ciepliński, whom I valued for the mild skepticism he brought to his teaching.

"Sir, why don't Polish schoolchildren learn things that are really worth the effort, and instead they're forced to cram their heads full of second-rate material?"

"What's all this, Gombrowicz? What are you taking about?"

"It's very simple. In our Polish classes we have to cram up on Mickiewicz and Słowacki and Krasiński, who from the perspective of general literature are entirely second-rate—to say nothing of Towiański.

At the same time we know nothing whatsoever about Shakespeare, or Goethe for instance. We waste time studying the wars with the Turks, but we're almost completely ignorant about the history of Europe or of the world. And what about Latin vocabulary? Because of it, there's no time for us to actually find out about Rome or Greece, and we don't really have any idea of the culture of that time. What's the value in such an education?"

"Gombrowicz may have something of a point. School could pay a little more attention to universal culture. But please don't forget that we are Poles."

"What of it?"

"Gombrowicz is forgetting that not so long ago Żeromski and his colleagues were persecuted for speaking Polish at school."

"So what? Because of that we have to be only half-educated?"

How well I hear, after all these years, the sarcastic, scornful tone with which I uttered the word *half-educated*. I wanted nothing to do with sentimentalities from the times of bondage, nor patriotic motivations. I demanded enlightenment and education based not on Poland's modest contribution to world culture, but on the most notable universal human values. To this day I hold to such a belief. It's not healthy when one's homeland becomes a screen that blocks out the rest of the world—it's not healthy even for the homeland itself. But at the time I was unaware that the educational systems of other countries are no less insular than Poland's.

It would seem, for example, that Argentina, which has only 150 years of history and has not experienced major problems in retaining its independence, could permit itself a broader, more universal program. Far from it! The less history a country has, the more they teach it in the schools to make up. They have their great men, their so-called *proseres,* but of many of them it could be said that any port in a storm will do. The net result is that the average Argentinian, whose head is filled with local generals, has only the faintest idea about the rest of humanity. Fortunately Argentinian literature leaves much to be desired, which forces them to read foreign books. We Poles suffer additionally from having a decent literature, one that is good enough to fill the hours we devote to reading, but not good enough to compensate for the resulting lack of familiarity with the great writers of the world, whom we no longer have time to study.

I suspect that Polish schools today are little different in this regard from those of forty years ago. So what if, as I imagine, Latin with its majestic foolishness has been removed from the schedule, and more hard sciences and technical classes have been added? School should not merely aim to produce engineers and lawyers, but to create people who have some kind of orientation toward the world and toward humanity. Do students have, for example, any kind of understanding of contemporary thought, not in a narrow, professional way but in the broadest and most profound sense? Do they know something of Kant, Schopenhauer, Nietzsche, Hegel? Are they familiar with the name of Kierkegaard; have they heard of surrealism? Are they familiar with the great intellectual currents that created Europe? Or is their knowledge restricted to Poland and to practical concerns?

Unfortunately Marxism, instead of opening students' minds to the world, closed them off even more hermetically. Lessons in dialectical materialism are very similar to the lectures on religion in Jesuit schools of the eighteenth century—a single doctrine is given as the one highest truth, and in this way Marxism has become an iron curtain cutting people off from all the other achievements of Europe. Marx was a clever man and a good European—that is, until he was served up by the Marxists. The provincial nature of Russo-communist thinking, attributing every invention ever made to the Russians and marked by a childish arrogance, must also have some influence on Polish schooling.

According to UNESCO statistics from 1953, Polish schools require a considerable effort on the part of the student: 212 school days per year, and 6,840 hours in the classroom. In the United States the figures are 180 days and 5,400 hours, and in Belgium 200 days and

4,800 hours. For myself, if I learned anything at all in school, it was more likely to be in the breaks, from my schoolmates as they beat me up. Other than that, I educated myself by reading books, especially those that were forbidden, and by doing nothing—for the freely wandering mind of the loafer is that which best develops the intelligence. For this reason, I'm not impressed by the huge number of hours spent in school, which deprive students of a personal life. And if on top of it all those hours are filled with unintelligent, narrow lessons aimed exclusively at producing a professional with the automatic soul of a Marxist, we have no choice but to become an uneducated nation.

At this time, certain forms were dying out that until recently had been full of life . . . something that I observed with the savage delight of a young stripling galloping into the future. Thus, honor was dying out, the old-fashioned kind of honor, solemn and forbidding, with its seconds, its top hats, its pistols and protocols. Good manners were inflexible. If you began a conversation in the train, after a few exchanges you had to stand and present yourself: "I am X. Permit me to introduce myself." There was a story I enjoyed from the time of my childhood that I hope is no longer current: A certain gentleman visits a public bathroom and realizes too late that there is no paper. Without a second thought he pokes his head over the wall to the next stall and says, "Allow me to introduce myself. I'm X. Could I ask for some paper?" Upon which the gentleman in the next stall also pokes his head over, and says, "I'm Y. Pleased to make your acquaintance. Here you are." I truly hope that this anecdote is no longer in fashion amongst you, though I wouldn't bet my life on it.

One kissed women's hands, and at larger gatherings one could observe men planting one kiss after another on hands reaching out from the sofa. It was the dying days of wing collars, gaiters, canes, striped pants, tail coats, frock coats, and innumerable other things. Honor would still sometimes find a bloody manifestation. A certain officer refused to show the conductor his tram ticket. "You don't trust the word of a Polish officer?" he asked, frowning, and he started shooting when the conductor called a policeman. I expect that today honor has relaxed somewhat (not too much, I hope); but I'm not at all certain that proletarian Poland has cured itself of ceremoniousness. The lady engineers and lady lawyers who visit from Poland still appear rather formal alongside the Argentinians with their easy ways, and their manner of expressing themselves is still marked by a mania for titles, though these are now bourgeois and bureaucratic rather than noble in character.

When certain customs are on the wane, they succumb to a kind of sclerosis; they lose their living core, and what remains is merely the stiffness of "pure form," as Witkiewicz would have put it. Now, I found myself fascinated by this formalism. It galled me, but also entranced me artistically. My work is filled with such dying forms; for instance, there are several scenes involving duels, not to mention other rituals of the gentry and the aristocracy. And these abrupt transformations in ways of being increasingly called my attention to the role of form in life, the powerful influence of gesture and mien on our innermost essence. I think I experienced this so intensely because I happened to enter life at a moment when the dying forms of that departing era still had some vitality and could bite. For example, at school, we would administer proud and resounding slaps in the face to one another, though they wouldn't end in a duel. The insulted party had to "respond" in kind if he were not to be dishonored—but then his opponent in turn had to "respond," since an unwritten rule declared that the last one to smack the other in the gob was the winner. Once, Tadzio Kępiński and I twice crossed the entire playground while smashing each other in the mug; my face became horribly swollen, and so did his.

They were strange, these prehistoric relics from an old, finished time at large in the new democracy that was becoming more all-embracing with every day. But anachronisms dragged on in places till the last years of the interwar period, and occasionally they exploded in an extraordinary burst of eccentricity. I remember that in 1936 or 1937 my brother asked me to hire a steward for his property in the country. A handful of candidates appeared at the designated time; amongst them was a blond young man who conveyed to me via the maid a very distinguished-looking visiting card bearing an aristocratic name and a coat of arms. After a short conversation it became clear that he did not possess the necessary qualifications. At this point he stood up and asked for his card back. "I'm sorry?" I said. "Please return my card to me," he said. I looked for it, but the accursed card had gone missing. "I won't leave till you give me my card back!" "What do you need it for?!" "That card has my coat of arms on it, and I can't be sure that you'll treat it with respect. I will not allow my coat of arms to be thrown in the trash, or worse!" Realizing that I was inches away from an affair of honor, I crawled under all the furniture in the immediate vicinity and in the end, luckily, I found the card.

In that time rich in changes, one of the most significant transformations was the abolition of men's facial hair. Not just beards, but mustaches too disappeared. This was a huge, powerful change, given that a man with a beard or a mustache is an entirely different sort of person from a clean-shaven man. I'm inclined to think that the consequences of this alteration were immeasurable—in art, in morality, in customs, even in politics, in metaphysics even—if not hard to understand. I'll never forget the shriek that my cousin gave when she saw my father walk into the apartment completely clean-shaven—he had just left his beard and mustache behind at the barber's, in keeping with the spirit of the times. This was the terrified scream of a woman whose deepest modesty had been offended. She couldn't have made more of a commotion if my father had been utterly naked. And in fact she was right, for it truly was shamelessness of the first order, that face of my father's, hitherto covered in hair and now for the first time scandalously exposed.

That was exactly how the face of the age was starting to appear to us striplings; and my already rather sensitive tastes told me distinctly that certain actions and opinions were "in the spirit of the age," others not, and that, for those other actions and opinions, this meant the death sentence. Although I frequently descended, as it were deliberately, into various anachronisms—such as the snobbishness I have mentioned—love of my era was very strong in me, and alongside it a feeling of solidarity with my generation. I once spoke about this here in America with a Central American writer of my age, and he confessed to the same weakness, even expressing it vividly. "At that time, for my generation I would have sacrificed my own father," he said. Why was it that even America in those years experienced the lure of history, which today's youth do not know? Because that age was a liberating age, an era filled with promise, and not just for us Poles. It was only later that there came blows, one after another, and everything began to subside into blood, pain, tedium, and crushing grayness. We didn't know then that in two of the empires brought down by the war there already simmered the makings of a new catastrophe.

Of all the circles, styles, and spirits that were coming to an end after the First World War, the most magnificent in its dying days was the landed gentry, the spirit of the petty nobility. It was an imposing spirit that only yesterday had ruled the country; it had been molded by tradition and polished by literature, and it contained all the beauty of Polishness. What a sight it was to see the gentry, all kind-hearted, good, plump, insular folk, suffering so painfully as everything began to shrink around them and forced to face up to modernity armed only with a few clichés from Weyssenhof and Sienkiewicz! It was capital entertainment for a youthful sadist. With great relish I began to indulge in provocations in various manors and country houses around Sandomierz and Radom. The workers' movement was not yet of any interest to me; I hadn't yet come into contact with communism, and I didn't believe in socialism—from the first encounter it had seemed to me nothing but mawkish idealism.

My high school graduation exams were approaching. I found myself in rather troublesome circumstances, since for some years now I had barely even opened my schoolbooks; during the lessons I practiced ever more perfect forgeries of teachers' signatures, both with and without flourishes, and I was promoted from one class to the next more by good luck than good judgment. As early as the fourth grade Principal Jaczynowski gave me a dressing down because I would come to school without my books and carrying only a small notebook. I responded to this accusation by hiring a messenger—such messengers would stand on the street corner in those days—who entered the school with me, bearing a knapsack with my books.

Kazio Baliński and Antoś Wasiutyński were good at math, and they sat in the front row. It was to them I was indebted for cribs and for whispering the answer during tests. In other, less terrible matters I was saved by my native quick-wittedness, my eloquence, and my exceptional talent for distracting the teacher's attention. But life was a string of Ds, and though I only once ever had to repeat a class—in Latin—I was an inferior student and tried only to achieve the minimum needed to advance to the next class at the end of the year.

The day when the entire truth about schooling is revealed—a day that is still very far off—humanity will find itself looking at a massive hoax and a colossal imposture. At that time it will come to light that teachers prattle on and students do not listen; that no one does anything; that students deceive and teachers allow themselves to be deceived; and that if one put one's mind to it, thirty hours of intensive study would be enough for three terms of the present school system. School in its current form is excellent preparation—but only for the life of a clerk, for bureaucratic time-wasting and make-believe work. This drawn-out, long-winded, bureaucratic, apathetic schooling is the very opposite of true learning, which is compact, intense, electrifying.

A few months before the graduation exams I realized the precariousness of my situation. It had been years since I had studied systematically; I hadn't the faintest idea about Latin, algebra, or trigonometry, while in other subjects I was a prize dunce. I was faced with five written exams and eight orals. What was I to do? As a consistent idler I decided to do nothing at all, particularly because there was in fact nothing that *could* be done beyond commending myself to the care of the Almighty. And so the fatal day came, in April, I believe, 1922. We all took our seats in the largest hall in the school, each on a separate bench so as to prevent cheating, and in deathly silence we were given the topic for our Polish essay. I wrote a lot and was quite pleased with myself. The real tragedy began the following day, when a sheet of paper appeared on my desk bearing a Latin text that was to be translated. Glancing at these few sentences, I realized that I knew nothing, I understood nothing, I had no desire to know anything, and that I was incapable of translating even three words. The deathly silence persisted. I was alone on my bench, in front of this idiotic sheet of paper, alone with that fake Latin: Never before had a murderous, killing sense of the absurd struck me with such force.

The same thing happened, alas, in the written math exam. My mathematical ineptitude made itself glaringly felt. I attacked the trigonometry exercise with the boldness of a desperate man—and to my astonishment, in ten minutes I had solved it. Everything worked out so neatly that all I had to do was to add up some figures, and it was done. But I knew this was too good to be true, and so in consternation I sought alternative solutions, to no avail. Each time I tried, like a train on a dead-end track I would find myself with the same, ever-so-simple, ever-so-smooth, blindingly evident solution. In the end I yielded—it was impossible to resist the obvious—and, plunged in darkest forebodings, I turned in my notebook. I knew I was headed for an F; but what was I to do if my work was faultless? Yes, an F in trigonometry, an F in algebra, and an F in Latin—these three letters crowned my efforts. I appeared to be beyond help.

But for my Polish essay I received an A plus. And in French, a language I had learned rather well at home, I also got an A plus. The examination committee was dumbfounded and decided to send my file to the ministry, where a favorable verdict was returned: I had passed.

We celebrated our high school graduation in the apartment of Miecio Grabiński, known as "the Chairman"; he lived on Jerozolimska Street, opposite the main railroad station. I got drunk, along with everyone else, and threw up from the windows of the sixth floor onto the street; but in my addled state I failed to notice that there was a café there, with tables on the sidewalk. The roar that went up from below induced me to hurriedly alarm my companions, and we barricaded the door, prepared to defend ourselves to the bitter end.

That summer I spent in Sopot on the Baltic. What should I study at university? Truth be told, nothing really appealed to me. Perhaps philosophy a little; but even then I had understood that to know something about philosophy one should go to the bookstore, buy a few books, and read them, instead of wasting time on lectures and seminars. Consequently, I chose the subject most convenient and attractive to shirkers: law. In the fall I began to attend the lectures on Roman law given by Professor Koschembar-Łyskowski.

Soon, however, I stopped actually going to the university. Law proved to be inhumanly tedious, and my fellow students were not especially interesting either. When I read Żeromski's journals of his university years—colorful, abundant in friendships, politics, dreams, poetry and other outpourings, so full of what he calls that "brilliant student chatter"—I envy him. Fate denied me such enthusiasms. It's a strange thing: Although Żeromski matured very quickly and in his early twenties sported a beard and had a good few broken hearts under his belt, not to speak of other experiences, I, a pup and a milksop in comparison with him, was nevertheless in another way much more mature. My maturity manifested itself in the conviction that "life is life," as my uncles in the country would say, and that no reforms, campaigns, movements, or struggles could bring my colleagues an ounce more sense, or turn the earth into a paradise. I was a realist through and through; I abhorred illusions, slogans, and paper theories. I loathed enthusiasm.

There is a saying—I don't know who coined it—that "at twenty, one is an arsonist; at forty, a firefighter." For better or for worse—most likely for worse as far as my personal life was concerned—around the age of twenty I was already one of the firefighters, and it was with a skeptical smile that I listened to the rousing speeches and songs of the students, restless as they have always been through history. Today I don't hold it against myself. Not to possess that physical and intellectual boisterousness doesn't mean to be soft or compliant—the English are proof of this—and it's possible to be perfectly aware of all the worthlessness of our inflammable credulity, and also of the utter severity of life, and at the same time to hold firmly to what one considers to be important values. I may have already been troubled by a foretaste of the coming bankruptcy, a secret conviction that glass houses are doomed to receive a shattering kick from a hobnailed boot. I didn't take part in the independence celebrations; I kept my distance, and when, on the street, I was overtaken by the sounds of a military march and the rhythmic tread of a passing army unit, I tried not to march in step. Was I perhaps searching for my own music and my own march? The problem with this was that I had no notion of what to turn my hand to. What should I be? Lawyer? Judge? Money-grubber? Professor? Philosopher? Artist? Gentleman farmer? Each of these roles was within my grasp, yet none of them was particularly to my liking.

In one respect I resembled my generation: I was unable to find "my own" reality. I picked up one book after another and said: "This isn't it." I read newspapers of every political stripe and said, "This isn't it."

In the fall of that year I fell ill with a lung ailment. Only the upper part of the lungs was affected, and I had just a slight temperature in the evening hours, but my mother was concerned and decided to send me to the country. My brother Janusz had recently married, and his wife owned a property in Iłżec province called Potoczek. The manor house was situated in woods in which there was a chain of five lakes stretching for several kilometers as far as the village—a truly Weyssenhoffian landscape. My brother and his wife were living at

Małoszyce at the time and rarely visited Potoczek. It was decided that I should spend the whole winter there, in that resin-soaked atmosphere. As I set off I had no idea what to expect.

A house in the woods is always a little melancholic. But a house in the woods where there's no one around, where dusk falls undisturbed by anything, where night is really night along with all its frenzy, the desperate yapping and howling of dogs . . . True, I was not alone. I had been left a cook, who fed me magnificently and fattened up my meager bones; I also had a young manservant, Bolek, at my disposal, and in addition there were a few local girls bustling about in the kitchen. Yet I was alone, all alone, for this was not company for me. For obvious reasons I couldn't permit myself any eccentricities, nor any familiarity. I couldn't "demoralize" the staff, and I had to behave with discretion. The "young master" would sit at the table, where there awaited him, for instance, fish in jelly; he would drink a glass of vodka, exchange a few words along the lines of, "How are you, Bolek; did you see how much snow fell in the night?", and in the afternoons he would set off for the woods with a shotgun. I ate till I thought I would burst. It was hot in the house. The servants did what they could for me. I got bored and ate; ate and rambled about the woods; returned home and ate some more; went to bed and listened to the sudden hullabaloo of the dogs, the fearful sounds of the night, and the even more frightening silence, interspersed with the murmur of the pines.

In fact, I did have something to do: I was writing a paper on *Solidarity* by the French sociologist Léon Bourgeois, for a seminar. But all that sociology bored me, and I quickly abandoned it. What was I to do? I felt a deep-seated disquiet, a growing sense that something was not as it should be with me in this manor house—that I was staying in bed too long, that I had to do something to justify my existence and put an end to this sybaritism, which was beginning to stifle me. I was feverishly seeking a way out—looking to take something on, to act, to purify myself through exertion—but what was I

to do? The snowy quiet of the surrounding trees was the only response. And in the end, exasperated, almost in despair, and not
knowing which way to run or where to hide, I began to sketch out a
novel—about a certain bookkeeper—and I was gradually drawn in
and began working on it systematically.

It was strange, toxic work. For a beginning writer everything is
difficult—saying the simplest thing, for example "she sat down and
asked for a glass of water," can become a problem for him. Consequently, as I wrote I sighed and groaned in the constant effort to hoist
my prose up to the level of art, where it would become vibrant and
lustrous. I worked harder than a wagon driver or a cook, and so my
conscience was cleansed; nevertheless, despite this the work was
somehow suspect, phony. It was tough, and produced with a struggle;
yet it didn't inspire respect. This was my first encounter with the
shame that accompanies any artistic labor, especially the kind that
has not won the approval of others and is not in demand. That shame
would weigh heavily upon me for many, many years; it was only recently that it began to ease up a little.

The work that was coming to life in such agonies was extremely
ungainly. I not only lacked the early talents of Krasiński, who wrote
The Un-Divine Comedy at the tender age of twenty; my inner uncouthness, my lack of literary sophistication, all my agitation and
coarseness deprived me even of the polish that is easily acquired by
any young person who spends time in literary circles.

I read an excerpt to my brother and his wife when they came to
visit me.

"It's atrocious," said Janusz. "Throw it away—it's an embarrassment. Don't tell anyone what you've done, and in the future find
something different to occupy your time."

And my sister-in-law, who was known as Pifinka, commented,
"It's a pity you didn't go hunting more often."

In my heart I knew they were right. I burned my work and took up
my sociology once again. But that first attempt of mine indicated

that in the solitude of Potoczek the poisons which had long been troubling me were making themselves felt ever more insistently. And soon after my brother and his wife visited, a bizarre thing occurred to which I ascribe a significant influence on my mental life.

This is what happened: One night I woke up with the sensation of a weight on my legs. I guessed it must be the large dog that would sometimes find its way into the living quarters from the kitchen. It had obviously climbed onto my bed. I kicked it off and called out, "Scat!" The dog growled and left, though I couldn't see it because everything was dark.

At that very moment, however, I was seized by a ghastly suspicion—no, almost a certainty—that it hadn't been a dog, but a creature a hundred times more terrible. I was alone in the house; there was nothing but the creak of the well outside in the wind, and the drip of melting snow from the roof. There was a full moon, but nearly all its light was kept out by the drapes. Rigid with fright, I tried to explain to myself that I had no justification in thinking the dog had not been an ordinary dog; but, as always at such times, a question immediately came to me: "If that's so, then why did the idea impose itself on me, why did it cling to me so forcefully? There must be something to it for me to be afraid for no apparent reason."

I didn't sleep a wink till dawn; but the daytime brought no relief either. I was still haunted by my experience. Something lay behind that dog; it meant something terrifying yet unknown. I couldn't figure out what it was. I spent several days and nights like this, as if on the verge of learning some awful secret, but unable to lift the curtain.

At last enlightenment came! A light was suddenly lit in my mind!

I remembered. Had someone told the story in my presence when I was a child, or was I myself there at the scene? Bishop Ryx of Sandomierz was once a guest of my parents', and he confided that he'd been visited by an evil spirit when he was still a seminarist and was about to be ordained. In the night, he felt a weight on his legs. He kicked the dog off. The dog was unbelievably heavy and fell to the floor with a metallic noise. "In the light of the moon," recounted the bishop, "I saw not a dog but a tiny person, as if made of metal, perhaps eighteen inches high. I shouted, 'bless us all!', and the thing gave a shriek and hid under the wardrobe. Later it turned out that the floor in that place was charred. I ran out of the house, even though it was freezing cold, and spent the entire night under the stars."

Then everything was clear! This story had lodged in my subconscious and had filled the good mongrel that I had driven away with a diabolic essence. Yet today, I can see that this incident had far-reaching consequences for me. The days during which I lived in the shadow of that sinister enigma had led me into previously unknown regions of the mind, from which it was not at all easy to return to the regular path. They had put me in touch with the Mystery, the Mask; they had revealed to me the power of hidden meanings, uprooted me from the everyday and thrust me into pathos, into the drama of our true situation in the world. These almost dreamlike revelations showed me a powerful, sibylline language that I often strove to recapture in my subsequent artistic works.

*

About student life I have little to say since I hardly ever took part in it. As concerns the program of study in the law school, it came down to an insane two months of cramming before the exams, which had the advantage of all being held on a single day. After this exertion I could rest for ten months till a new test that would determine if I could advance to the next year.

So I studied very little, and rarely if ever appeared at the university, since attendance at lectures was not obligatory. I wonder whether this wise system of education, which allows students (who for the most part must work to earn their keep) to use their time most efficiently, continues to this day? Political life was equally uninteresting to me. Then how did I live? I was a passionate tennis player; I played some chess, devoted myself to reading, conversed with my friends. Such idleness! And yet it wasn't as absolute as things might have seemed. In those years I acquired, without knowing how, an intellectual ascendancy over those around me; it slowly emerged that I was more intelligent than they. How had this happened—thanks to what—was it so noticeable—and how did it jibe with my awkward manner and my various naiveties? Oh, I do not know; don't ask. Everything is lost in the host of everyday days; but it somehow became established that I was "intelligent," that my specialty was intelligence rather than anything else. I was very much flattered by this, and when my female cousins begged me, "explain this to me—you're so intelligent," I felt I was not completely bankrupt after all. Except that my intelligence was hanging from the ceiling, its feet kicking in the air without a point of support. What was worse, I myself had no place. I belonged neither to artistic nor intellectual circles. I was not in any group or any movement. I was supposedly a "citizen's son" from the country, but I had nothing in common with the country and could barely tell oats from wheat.

"When I visit my brothers," Jerzy was fond of saying, "I'm only afraid of one thing: that Janusz doesn't go to bed and that Witek doesn't start talking nonsense."

Talking nonsense was undeniably one of the occupations I found most absorbing in those times. But today may I be allowed to say that I am far from condemning that existence of mine, when I was left entirely to my own resources, with no ties to anyone, given to loafing, devoid of support, discipline, norms, and forms, inept and callow. I would even be inclined to believe that this existence was the supreme school for me—a kind of super-university which, imperceptibly, educated whatever it was in me that later enabled me to break out and find my way to the outside world. Human beings are social creatures, and those who blend into their environment quickly and smoothly will be successful and will acquire a high degree of competence; yet the source of their innermost energy will not sound within them. They will remain technically useful, but superficial and insular.

Since the stay in Potoczek hadn't cured me completely, I left to spend the summer in Rabka.

I recall that this stay in Rabka further exacerbated my (already strained) relations with other people. For in the bizarre guest house where I was staying, I found myself in the company of what seemed to be a deliberately chosen assortment of characters who together exemplified the Polish confusion of styles and Polish grotesquery. We ate at a common table, and not one of those individuals gathered around it was entirely genuine. The ladies were pretentious and affected, or else exaggeratedly modest, or melancholic and embittered, or domineering and exhaustingly dynamic. As for the gentlemen, none resembled any of the others and, aware of their differences and at the same time somewhat unsure of themselves, they were in a constant state of aggressive-defensive war, sniffing out allusions in everything—exactly like me myself. I immediately mobilized my complexes and became provocative, which soon led to rather unpleasant consequences.

One of these dames had a colossal advantage over the rest of us: She had spent several years in England, and so was "European." Her time in England ought to have taught her discretion and straightforwardness, but the opposite had happened. She tormented us at every meal with her Europeanness—and this was one of my complexes, for I had thus far been unable to resolve either Poland's attitude toward Europe or my own. In any case, in the end I could stand it no longer and said quietly but distinctly, "She's consumed so much of London that now it's repeating on her."

This was doubtless not a particularly witty or classy remark. It resembled me: It was heavy-handed and aggressive. But I didn't foresee the consequences. The Englishwoman gave me a withering stare and made some comment about bad-mannered whippersnappers. At this another gentleman, who was most authoritative and fearfully dignified, added a few words about the arrogance typical of foolish students, while another gentleman, something of a jokester, gave a high-pitched laugh. I kept my silence. I was miserable; I was a mixture of boorishness and extreme delicacy, and I was now paralyzed by this fact. And so I sat ill at ease, suddenly embarrassed. Then, as a result of the strange connections that are created in such circles, filled with idiosyncrasies, irritations, and eternal polemics, another gentleman, a retired judge, suddenly shouted at his daughter for playing cards before dinner and forbade her to do so again. "You have to know who you're playing with!"

These words engendered a new cataclysm that I didn't fully understand, though I assumed it was aimed at me. There was an icy chill. Everyone fell silent. And after dinner there was a stirring amongst the gentlemen—they too had taken part in the card game, and now they were offended and decided to demand an explanation. Each of them sent his proxies to the judge to ask what he had meant by saying, "You have to know who you're playing with." Eventually my turn came. Yet I was already thoroughly ill. I wasn't afraid of a duel, for there could be no question of one in this situation; but the combination of all this foolishness, the ghastly immaturity of all of us in this accursed guest house, left me in a dreadful state of helplessness, a tragic despondency. Enough! Enough! I no longer wished to participate in any of it. I felt utterly indifferent to it all. I didn't send my proxies to the judge, which of course discredited me in the eyes of the honor-conscious gentlemen; but I remained at the guest house for another two weeks, calm, cold, self-sufficient, indifferent, ah, almost unshaken in my role of tragic isolation. And solemn.

These were the kinds of leaps I made between clownishness and gravity, between playing the fool and real suffering. And all the while I was unable to cope with the whole Polish farce, with that disequilibrium of ours. It was an ocean in which I was drowning; yet I also carried it within myself. From Rabka I made a brief excursion to Zakopane; one evening, entering Trzaska's or Karpowicz's, at a table in the depths of the restaurant I spotted a familiar face: Boy-Żeleński!

I didn't know him personally, but I knew who he was: a writer, representing intelligence, talent, Europe. As I drank my tea I gazed at him from a distance. Perhaps I could go up to him? He was alone. The whole place was almost deserted. If I were to approach him, what would I say? I went up. "Mr. Żeleński?"

"That's right."

"Would you mind? I'd like just a couple of words with you . . . though we've not been introduced."

Boy-Żeleński was probably bored. He gestured toward a chair. "Be my guest."

I sat down and didn't know what to say. In the end I declared, "You know, I'm a passenger sitting on a chair; the chair is on a crate; the crate is on some sacks; the sacks are on a wagon; the wagon is on a ship; the ship is on the ocean. But where the land is and what kind of land it is, no one knows."

*

Boy-Żeleński looked at me with his somewhat sleepy, or perhaps dejected, gaze and said briefly, "Like all of us."

Someone else came up and that was the end of it. I reminded him of our conversation years later—it was just before the war, on his namesday if I remember correctly. He smiled and said, "We're sailing, sailing on that Polish ship, but we'll never feel solid ground beneath us—till we drown!"

*

When I was in my second year of law studies I set about writing another novel. But this work was entirely different in conception from the previous one about the bookkeeper that I had begun in the quiet of the Potoczek woods. This new adventure of mine with literature may have been as typical of my personal experiences of that time as it was of the general Polish cultural crisis—and so I will talk about it in some detail.

It began when Tadzio Kępiński, my former schoolfriend, and I decided to coauthor a thriller to make ourselves a pile of money. We didn't doubt that superior intellects like ours would have no problem producing such tripe—easy and gripping reading. Soon, however, we threw everything into the trash, dismayed at the gracelessness of our scribblings.

"Writing a bad novel doesn't seem to be any easier than writing a good one," I said at the time to Kępiński.

And this problem began to interest me. To create a good novel for the upper ten thousand, or even hundred thousand people—that can always be done, it's banal and tedious. But to write a good novel for lower, inferior readers, for whom what we call "good literature" is not to their taste . . .

"What does it mean, though, to say 'a good novel for the masses'?" I explained to Kazio and Zaza Baliński. "There's no reason why it has to be accessible and exciting and noble and refined, like Sienkiewicz or even Rodziewiczówna. A novel for the masses—one that is truly 'their' novel—should be made of what they really like, what they live by. It ought to appeal to their lowest instincts. It ought to be an outlet for a filthy, turbid, inferior imagination. It ought to be constructed of sentimentality, lust, stupidity. It ought to be dark and low."

Please don't be shocked. It was not so much contempt as fear that was speaking through me. Like all the Polish intelligentsia, I felt threatened by the primitiveness of the masses, which in Poland is much darker and more menacing than in countries where the culture is greater and above all more homogeneous. As we now know, this fear was not without foundation. But today I'm inclined to think that this idea of a "bad novel" was the high point of my entire literary career—I have never before or since been struck by a more creative notion. For what was the significance of that program, which at the time I was incapable of formulating clearly? However far removed he may be from the world, a writer always writes for someone, even if it's an imaginary reader. Of course one writes differently for an educated audience, or even for a critic, than for a common consumer of printed matter. But thus far, even when creating for tiny children, one always wrote "from above"—the writer did indeed descend to the level of the masses, but only insofar as his breeding and literary good manners permitted it.

In this sense my project was extraordinarily radical: to give oneself over to the masses, to become worse, lower—not only to describe that immaturity, but precisely to write through it. In a word, this was an ideal that in later life I was to define as the postulate that in culture not only should the lower be created by the higher, but the reverse too—the higher should be created by that which is low.

Those who from *Ferdydurke* and especially from my *Diary* are familiar with my, let us say, theory of form, which of course isn't restricted to artistic concerns but extends to the whole of humanity in all its manifestations—these people will be better placed to understand the audacity and radicalness of those intentions of mine. If it had come off, this book, written by a student, might have become the starting point for a revolutionary new literature and, who knows, may have opened up previously unknown regions of the mind, achieving something like the cocreation of two different phases of development. But what's the point of dreaming, as Rzecki used to say in *The Doll*. It did not come off, because the task was way beyond me, and moreover at the time I didn't realize its magnitude.

Nor its danger. . . . Here I shall add in parentheses that it was only ten years later I understood that I'd been playing with fire—a most unhealthy occupation. This was brought home to me by a certain visit. . . . Very well, I shall tell the story.

At the time I had already published my first book, *Recollections of Adolescence,* and in certain circles I was regarded as a bold and ultramodern writer. One morning the doorbell rings. It's a fair-haired young man in his twenties. He looks a little like a recruit, a little like the steward of a country estate; and under his arm he has a manuscript. "Please forgive my forwardness," he says, "but I've written a novel, and a friend of mine who knows about these things said I should show it to you. He says you may like it."

"Why's that?" I ask distrustfully, since the visitor's appearance gives no cause for special hopes.

"Well," he replies, growing increasingly nervous, "it's a novel . . . of an erotic character, you know. No holds barred! I deliberately allowed myself to write like that . . . so people would find it exciting—so they'd want to read it. Money's rather tight, I'm under my third eviction warning, you understand how it is? Please take a look," he adds by way of encouragement. "It's erotic!"

I took it and read it. With a growing sense of unease, distaste, pain even, because, yes indeed, it was erotic, and filthy, hopelessly filthy, infatuated with filth; on these pages there was nothing that purified. It was not only filthy, it was bad, it was cheap work, it was filthy trash. At times a description of filth can be found in literature, but it is so brilliant, so masterful, that the form redeems the content. Here, however, the very descriptions were contaminated with filth and incompetence. . . . Wait a moment: This reminded me of something—ah, that old novel of mine, long forgotten! I blushed, one might say mortally; and my stomach turned at the recollection!

He had left his telephone number. I called. "Can I speak with Mr. X?" There was whispering on the other end of the line. Finally the reply came, "He's not here." And eventually I learned that he had committed suicide. He had shot himself with a revolver, a week before.

Of course, I won't claim that it was because of the novel. Yet that work was an expression of the mental state that led him to disaster. And I realized that I too, ten years earlier, despite appearances, despite my almost carefree existence, was not so far from a similar decision; I, his fellow writer. Yes, I must have been deep in despair. . . . But first let us recount the fate of that masterpiece of mine. After a few months of work I finished it. It was a repulsive mixture of various outpourings—in sensuality, in violence, in cheap conquests, in second-rate mythology—a story no less slovenly and "exciting" than the awful novel by Mr. X. What was I to do with it? I died with shame at the thought of having to show it to anyone, but there was nothing for it; I wrote "for the reader" and had to be consistent. At the time I was staying in Zakopane and had gotten to know Mrs. Szuch, an intelligent and well-read person who valued me and believed in my abilities.

She returned the manuscript to me, refusing to look me in the eye, and said as if out of the corner of her mouth, "You should burn it."

I immediately went to my room, took the remaining copies from my suitcase, threw them all down in the snow outside the guest house, and set them on fire.

Why do I tell this story? And why do I remember my despair, and say that it was very Polish? In Poland, so-called refined people are not protected from the pressure of the masses by strong institutions, traditions, hierarchies, and the social order, as is the case in the West. In our country intelligence, delicacy, good sense, and talent are all helpless in the face of any kind of lowness originating in the social depths, out of squalor, out of eccentricity, barbarity, perversion and dissoluteness, out of ignorance and brutality. This is why our so-called intellectuals were and still are somewhat intimidated. The only thing that may have changed is that today the violence of the lower upon the higher is more organized.

The experience described above is unlikely to happen to a beginning writer in the West.

*

May 30, 1960

I was in the fourth year of my law studies when Piłsudski led an armed attack on the existing political system. I was no fan of Piłsudski and his ilk, perhaps partly because he was a man of the left, while my environment was conservative and did not trust the "mason," as he was known—a person, moreover, who was alleged to have organized hold-ups in post offices during the 1905 revolution! People would say: "Piłsudski? The man's a bandit!" But I wasn't especially susceptible to this kind of righteous indignation on the part of my uncles and aunts, and I probably would have enjoyed resisting it had it not been for another, more important consideration. The propaganda that was produced about him, the pompous adjectives that were applied to him, and the whole exalted and at the same time naive language of his followers—that was what grated on me.

Don't forget that I still possessed a little of the political good breeding which marked the departing age. People of those times expressed themselves more circumspectly and seriously; overly glaring falsehoods, bombast, excess, and servility were still something objectionable—unlike today, when no amount of commotion is capable of surprising anyone. It must be said too that the admiration of Piłsudski evinced by his adherents was child's play when compared to subsequent adorations at the shrine of Hitler, Mussolini, or Stalin. Piłsudski's people were above all soldiers who really did love their "Old Man"; but they were also often romantics steeped in the unwholesome fumes of Polish tradition and Polish art. And it was precisely this point that was hardest for me to swallow. Romanticism. Piłsudski too was a romantic who recited Słowacki and used to say of himself that "I am needed during the storm"—a typical exponent of eastern Polish mysticism who always struck me as suspect and dangerous.

What irritated me most, in later years, was Piłsudski's attitude to his own greatness. As is common knowledge, a great figure is one who has a will to rule, to dominate everyone else; a great figure seeks to be lord and master, whereas a romantic submits, withstands, suffers, and is the victim of the world, which is greater than him. The Marshal, then, who treated the Poles unceremoniously and imperiously, was nevertheless weighed down by Poland in its historical dimension, and even more so by his own mission—it impressed him, and he fell on his knees before Piłsudski the Leader, whom he bore within himself. The Old Man's brilliant realism—which sat ill in him alongside the poetry cooked up according to some eastern recipe that had turned his head—seemed to me an insufficient guarantee. Amongst his fans, in turn, all this frequently dissipated into a mist that entirely prevented clear-sightedness.

Then came the May morning when the cannon sounded. At the time we were living on Służewska Street and from the balcony I saw the military operations in the building of the Defense Ministry on what was then Nowowiejska Street. It was restricted to a few shots, but through the windows of the ministry one could see men moving along cautiously with rifles. I later learned that Sławoj-Składkowski had commanded this occupation of the ministry by Piłsudski's supporters. On the streets there was a lot of shooting, and on the Aleje Ujazdowskie, a few hundred yards away, there was a real battle with the military college, which refused to surrender.

As always at historic moments, nothing was clear and no one had any idea what was going on. History treats people not just cruelly but mockingly. Finally the storm died down and it was possible to go back on the streets, filled with a still-frightened public.

I first went to see my uncle, Władysław Sołtan, who was the governor of Warsaw province and lived close by on the Aleje; I thought I would learn something there. I learned nothing except some words spoken, I forget whether by Sołtan or his wife, which I often recalled later: "The Great Improvisation has begun."

The May upheavals, which shook the whole country, were not enough to bring me out of my isolation. I was still unable—and this inability was more powerful than I—to live the Polish collective life, either in politics or in culture. I watched from the sidelines, sometimes with interest, sometimes with passion—but take part? No. Absolutely not. Why? I was still too young to be fully conscious of my reasons, but I already knew a thing or two. A few years later it was clarified for me much more vividly when, on a hunting trip near Potoczek, I happened to meet a highly-placed colonel who at the time was a minister and was regarded as the leading intellect of the regime.

He drank my health most politely and, taking my arm, asked, "I know you have literary interests and that you're intelligent. Why do you hold yourself aloof?"

I'd already had a few glasses and was thereby inclined to a greater frankness than I would have been capable of sober. Holding a small plate with a sandwich in one hand and my glass in the other, I replied proudly, "Because I don't believe in any of it."

He looked at me in surprise.

"Who don't you believe in? The Marshal?"

"I believe in the Marshal," I replied. "But what can he do in the situation in which he finds himself?"

"What do you mean by that? The situation? What situation? The situation is not at all bad. There's nothing threatening us."

"On the contrary," I answered. "The situation is terrible; so terrible that even if the Marshal were Bismarck and Talleyrand all rolled into one there's nothing he could do. It's all useless, you understand?"

The eminent colonel began talking with someone else. Did this mean I had been visited by a prophetic spirit and could foresee the coming disasters? Not a bit of it! But I did have a vague feeling that "something was rotten," and that everything smacked of shoddiness and a patch-up job. I couldn't bring myself to see it all as solid work, though Poland after the coup was in many respects a pleasant place that showed great promise for the future. The state had been strengthened, certain anachronisms had been eliminated, and our antique order from before the war, built around the nobility, was slowly becoming transformed into a democratic system, while the working classes were assuming ever more importance. Only someone whose mind was on the moon could have demanded that a country recently born upon the corpses of three empires should overnight become a model of modern democratic organization.

I wasn't blind, and I could see that despite everything we were somehow moving forward. And yet it was still all so flimsy! The flimsiness was lurking underneath; it wasn't possible to undertake anything fundamental, but instead everything had to be temporary, circumspect; one should just patch things over, wait and see. No bold or radical initiatives could survive in these conditions, and outstanding people like Piłsudski were doomed to indistinctness.

Once I was talking with a corn merchant in Ostrowiec whose son was a poet.

"So, Mr. Szlomo, why didn't you join Seidenbeutl in that venture of his?"

"I would've done, sir, but this whole lackadaisical system doesn't give any room for new ideas to spread their wings."

This was the reason I stood to the side in Polish political, social, and cultural life—it did not give one room to spread one's wings. Within this was concealed the germ of the future disaster that utterly distorted our chances for growth and condemned us to stagnation.

Was this egotism on my part? Coldness? I think I may still have been too young to be judged so harshly. Later on a great deal within me changed.

*

I finished my law degree. At the final examination in civil law an astonishing thing happened that can only be compared to a large win in the lottery. After a few questions that I managed somehow or other to bumble through, the professor said to me, "Please find this clause in the statute book." I had never even seen the statute book before and had no idea whether I should look for the clause near the beginning or near the end. I thought to myself, It's over; but I opened the book at random. And guess what? I opened it right at that clause, even though the book was a big fat one with ever such thin pages. The professor said, "I see you're thoroughly familiar with the statute book." I replied, "Dear Lord!"

I had finished my studies; what was I to do? I had no desire whatsoever to be a lawyer or a judge. I was heartily sick of the law, especially because at the times when its subtlety and precision came into contact with real life there occurred a bogus sort of quid pro quo.

In theory it was a moment of exactness and logic; in practice criminals were dealt with in a rush, any old how, just to have done with them and to be able to move on. In the end I had come to loathe this pretentious knowledge, so vulgarly exposed for what it was by the lives that sat in the jury box.

Besides, at that time I had already begun to write short stories, and I had other things on my mind. But it was already essentially established in my family that I would travel abroad to pursue further studies in Paris, and I was not so crazy as to put up any resistance. By all means I could go to Paris, the more so because these studies allowed me to further put off my military service, which I was terribly afraid of.

One night, then, I set off on a pilgrimage into the heart of Europe—me, on the face of it a country bumpkin, an unmannered student, a provincial figure, and yet deep down so closely connected with this continent. The journey across Germany and Belgium, two nights and one day, was not particularly onerous, since I spent it using my broken German to romance the charming Gretchen, who had boarded the train in Berlin and got out in Brussels.

At last I found myself in the early morning at the Gare du Nord. I laughed to myself when from a speeding taxicab I caught sight of the Arc de Triomphe—it was already so familiar to me. I reached my small hotel near the Place de L'Etoile and flung myself on my bed. To hell with Paris—I wanted to sleep. It was only in the evening that I went out and began to walk about the streets.

If I wished to sum up my stay in Paris in a few words, that above all would be it—walking the streets. Not even roaming. Walking. I suspect there are few people who have seen less of Paris than I have. I visited nothing and was interested in nothing.

I had two contacts in the city: my cousin Bebuś Rosset, an officer in the 1st Uhlan Regiment, who occasionally painted and occasionally moved in Bohemian circles; and Janek Baliński, the son of the senator, brother of my friends Kazio and Zaza, and also a friend of mine. I went to visit him. He was living on the avenue Wagram in the apartment of some famous professor, one of those involved with the League of Nations. Janek spent his time arranging international collaborations as the president or delegate of Polish youth organizations. Baliński, an ardent admirer of the West and of France, tried to share his enthusiasm with me, but his zeal abated when he realized I showed no interest. Things didn't work out with Rosset either. He received me in a romantic garret with a view of spires and rooftops; as if it were yesterday I remember that as I entered his hallway from the stairs, he was filling his kettle from the faucet.

"Oh, you're here," he said. "Well, I suppose we'll have to do something with you. I hear you write? Do you want to be a *pisarz* (writer) *polonais?*" (I'd rather not explain this play on words.) "I'll introduce you to my friends."

And nothing came of this either. He threw a party that was attended by a few painters, an occupation for which I've never had much fondness, and a few writers who were also not exactly fully fledged. The brotherhood looked me over sniffily. They were right to do so, since next to these Bohemians I had become even more reserved, stiff, phlegmatic, and bourgeois—a veritable milksop! The principal reason for this was probably my loathing of stereotypes—this Parisian-ness, unkempt and tieless, was just too hackneyed and, precisely in Paris, insufferable. But pride also played a part, for I didn't wish to look artistically disheveled *avant la lettre,* before I had become an actual artist. Besides, to this day, among artists I like to behave like a bourgeois, and with the bourgeoisie like an artist, just to annoy people. In any case, I failed the examination, and when Bebuś insisted that I leave my respectable quartier and move into his building, I refused, and Bebuś lost interest and left me to my own fate.

Bebuś was an uncommonly bold man, with a rich and stormy nature, whom war dislodged from his normal life. His death was violent and strange, indiscreet even. He fell in love unhappily with a certain lady and at one point arranged a meeting with her at the Café de l'Opéra for a deciding conversation. They sat down at a table. The woman said no. At once he took out a revolver and there in the crowded café, as they sat together at the table, he shot himself in the head.

As I recall, the following spine-chilling story also involves him. At the time he was serving as the military attaché in our embassy in Ankara. Once, when he was taking part in a séance, the glass began to tap out a message in Russian: "I shall visit you in the night." He took this to refer to himself, since no one else present spoke Russian or had dealings with Russians, whereas he had killed many of them during the war with the Bolsheviks in 1920. He returned home and went to bed. In the night he woke up and felt someone lying next to him. He reached out and touched a body that was cold as ice, cold as a corpse. He leapt out of bed and ran out into the street.

But I shall return to my Parisian adventures.

At the Graduate Institute for International Studies where I was enrolled, there were many interesting young people from all over the world—but what of it, since I rarely showed my face in that august school. I was tired of studying. What should I do? Visit Paris? I couldn't face all that standing about in front of churches with head tipped back, all those pilgrimages to museums. I once went into the Louvre, stared at a couple of paintings and one statue, and breathed a sigh of relief when I found myself back outside, in the sun, far from that deathly silence and that smell. Then what should I do? I walked about the streets, not any particular streets and not to soak up the Parisian atmosphere. I walked like a person who has nothing to do, and only from time to time does something catch his attention—a voice, a smile, a gesture, a view of a street, a store sign. But eventually the day came when I met a certain Chinese . . .

At the time I was strapped for cash and I stopped in for supper at a very shabby little restaurant on the Boulemiche. As I waited for my steak I tried to tap out something from Bach's Third Brandenburg Concerto on the tabletop, when suddenly I noticed that at the next table an Asian gentleman was evidently wrestling in the same way with the First Brandenburg Concerto. We exchanged knowing glances.

"Do you like music?"

The Chinese man was known as Hsu, though in reality his name was more complicated; he was studying philosophy and literature at the Sorbonne, and previously for a year he had been a student of Alan's. His parents, who he said were very rich, owned plantations and factories; but he'd had a mortal falling-out with them, and he had no intention of returning to China. After supper we went for a long walk, which has stuck in my memory: I can see us crossing the slippery asphalt of the Place de la Concorde, recently washed by the rain, and talking, talking, talking. . . . It was the beginning of one of the most important dialogues of my life.

*

July 4, 1960

You know already, then, that while I was in Paris for my studies in 1928, I visited nothing and was interested in nothing, and my entire stay was really no more than idle walking on the Parisian sidewalks. Just to kill time. When I mention this here, Argentinians who for years on end have been saving up for a pilgrimage to the Ville Lumière simply gnash their teeth.

Yet this indifference to Paris was only a pose. Deep down, it was an implacable war, and this struggle of mine with Paris broke out, strange to relate, because of Hsu, the Chinese man, whom I had met by chance in a little student restaurant on the Boulemiche when we were both returning from a Bach concert. This Hsu, who was affectionately called *mon choux,* took me to one of the cafés in the vicinity of the Panthéon and introduced me to his companions. Why did I pay no attention at the time to their names? I'm certain many of them have distinguished themselves today. Those young people were edgy, lively, impetuous, and sharp, and they expressed themselves brilliantly. The majority were French, but there were also Italians, Rumanians, Spanish, and the requisite American women, as well as representatives of more exotic countries.

There were even a few priests who would come, I suspect more for the enjoyment of the discussion than to try to win over unbelievers.

I behaved with immense reserve. My instinct told me not to stand out and not to show off. I was glad when I was sometimes mistaken for an Englishman. But one night an altercation took place between me and them.

"Do you like Paris?"

"I suppose so. To be honest, I've hardly visited anything."

"Why's that?"

"I don't like craning my neck in front of buildings, and in general sightseeing bores me and depresses me."

After some time the topic came up again.

"So Paree hasn't met with your approval?"

"To be honest, not really . . . not much."

"Why's that? You don't like the views from the Place de la Concorde?"

A couplet of Boy-Żeleński's came to mind: "Today, the better manners one puts on, / The more one blushes at one's own salon."

I translated it into French. I truly had the requisite respect for all the Gothic and Renaissance. It was just a pity that the people were not up to it, *à sa hauteur.* Frankly, the Parisians were rather unprepossessing and devoid of charm and . . .

By this point I was being shouted down. Parisians devoid of charm!

"That's right," I replied. "That's right. Alas! They're only too aware that they are bewitching and that Paree is delightful. That whole French esprit—how intrusive it is! Nor am I a fan of Parisian taste. These ladies' fashions don't appeal to me—they're excessive, over-stylized. The ladies themselves look like they're from a fashion magazine, with their garish lipstick. Paris lacks cleanliness and freshness. And all that art of yours is somehow foolish. And all your amour, this

Parisian love, is just some middle-class, dressing-gowned manipulation that makes a person want to puke! This is a vomit-inducing city—there's nothing more to be said!"

This diatribe was received by the company with great delight. They liked passionate discussions, but as a rule they would be up to their ears in the intricacies of Bergson's philosophy, or anarchism. Here, however, was a stimulating topic and an opponent with whom one could have some fun. In a group of this kind there'll always be a specialist in the art of "puggery," that is, stirring things up; and I found myself in the clutches of a lanky fellow who looked like a younger, miniature Don Quixote.

"*Mais quand même! Mais c'est épatant!*"

My situation was unenviable: alone against a gang intent on mockery and very sure of themselves, alone with my provincial views, and in addition, with my command of French, which admittedly was not of the worst, but which couldn't keep up with their nimble and brisk speech. I realized that I had to be intelligent—that I could not permit myself an iota of unintelligence—that intelligence had to be expressed not only in my words, but in my very way of talking, of listening, of looking. The time had come to try out this slowly emerging Polish intellect of mine!

Instead of arguing with everyone, I addressed myself only to the native Parisians, ignoring the foreigners, and I expressed my astonishment that they could tolerate the atmosphere of inanity and snobbery that surrounds Paris. "In your place I'd go mad! How can you bear this idiotic delectation, mouth agape, nose in the air, these unbelievably hackneyed phrases, this snobbishness constantly reinforced by new waves of tourists, this estheticism of the very worst kind?!"

My maneuver turned out to be most effective. The students from other countries protested at once, irritated, which brought me even closer to the French; and in the space of a moment I was ensconced in their group, taking on the infuriated Rumanians and Turks. It didn't last long, but it allowed me to find a common understanding with them. Gradually, however, this game became ever more serious, and in the end we would come to the café as to a field of battle, in order to wage a conflict that had already lasted many days but was still far from being resolved.

For me this was extremely meaningful. As a Pole, a representative of a weaker culture, I had to defend my sovereignty: I could not allow Paris to get the better of me! And I realized in the course of these confrontations that what had prevented me thus far from enjoying Paris and taking advantage of it was precisely that: the necessity of maintaining my independence, dignity, and pride, the fear of becoming a pupil, an imitator, an acolyte, an admirer, a bystander. I attribute immense importance to those vehement debates in the tiny café on the Boulemiche, round the table in the corner. It was there, at this time, that I grasped the bull by the horns—a bull with which I was often to wrestle subsequently—the bull of western superiority.

I can still see it as if it were yesterday. There was a leather sofa against the wall on which some shop assistants, I believe, used to sit laughing at us and interrupting our conversation; a priest, abbé Barcelos, a Catalan and a poet, took part, though he sat aside, in effect at a separate table; while the six or seven of us, including the Chinese *mon choux,* would be talking, sometimes shouting, our heads off. On the other side of the street was a confectioner's from which one of our number would bring chocolates, obtained thanks to special connections and relations, which we would eat under the table so as not to be seen by Monsieur Vincent, who kept watch from behind the counter of our bar.

Dialectics are the mother of invention. It was then that I discovered the right way of polemicizing with Paris—a method that was and is urgently needed, and not by me alone. Listen to a conversation I had recently in the Argentinian city of Santiago del Estero with some students from the nearby university in Tucuman.

"Europe is crushing us culturally!" the students said. "It won't leave us alone! We don't want to imitate Europe! But we can't rebel because we're not mature. Yet we'll never attain maturity if we don't rebel. It's a vicious circle!"

"Not at all," I replied. "There's one very simple method. It's just that America hasn't hit upon it yet."

"What method?"

"It's the easiest thing in the world. Culture is not at all necessary in order to feel on an even footing, for instance with Paris. If you can't show maturity on a Parisian level, then you should simply try to show that Paris is as immature as you are! Let me show you that this is no paradox. What do you think: Where do people talk the most nonsense? In Paris or in Santiago?"

"Surely there can't be any doubt that it's in Santiago."

"Really? I would say the opposite. Because in Santiago people talk about concrete things, like harvests, or the behavior of your neighbor's daughter—things that are familiar to everyone. In Paris, on the other hand, they discuss existentialism, the music of Schönberg, or theoretical physics, which no one understands and which far exceed the abilities of the good Parisian bourgeoisie. In other words: Paris has more culture than Santiago, but it's precisely [one line missing in typescript].

*

My compatriots in Paris were less and less to my liking. I'd meet them from time to time, usually infrequently—a handful of students, or a few Polish families already half-gallicized. Once or twice I also took myself to the embassy and learned a lifelong lesson from those visits: that the ambassador's oysters should be avoided like tripe with oil, or like a hole in the head.

A couple of times I also attended events of the Parisian Polish community. I would leave exasperated, furious, vindictively malicious. It was a lot worse than could have been suspected, worse than anything that had irritated me in Poland—all those Cracovian dances, those Kościuszkos, those sentiments, those speeches, that ghastly habit of waving our "cultural achievements" in Europe's face!

Of course, I won't claim that we have no achievements—nor that they shouldn't be spoken about—but what bothered me was the way this was done, which revealed our awful inferiority complex and our lack of dignity—even our lack of a sense of humor.

For seven years I've been in the habit of recording in my writer's diary anything that irritates me or disturbs me. Once, for example, after an argument with Lechoń I poured out onto paper all the bile that I had accumulated concerning the Polish mania for self-promotion that I had first observed in Paris. Since my *Diary* is a forbidden book in Poland, I'll permit myself to quote a couple of passages that are very much connected with the experiences being described here. Listen:

> *I once happened to attend one of those meetings devoted to the mutual Polish fortifying and raising of spirits . . . where, after singing the Pledge and dancing a cracovienne, we set about listening to a speaker who glorified the nation because "we brought forth Chopin," because "we have Curie-Skłodowska" and Wawel Castle, and also Słowacki and Mickiewicz, and besides, we were the bulwark of Christianity and the Third of May Constitution was very progressive . . . He explained to himself and his audience that we are a great nation, which may not have stirred his listeners' enthusiasm (they were familiar with this ritual, and were taking part in it as they would in a church service, at which no surprises should be expected), yet nevertheless was received with a sort of satisfaction that a patriotic duty had been fulfilled.*

> *And I resented this confounded rite. . . . Because in raising up Mickiewicz, they abased themselves; and in praising Chopin they revealed precisely that they were not fit to hold a candle to him; and in relishing their own culture they exposed their own primitiveness.*

> *Geniuses? To hell with these geniuses! I felt like saying to those gathered:*

> *"What do I care about Mickiewicz? You're more important to me than Mickiewicz. Neither I nor anyone else will judge the Polish nation*

on the basis of Mickiewicz or Chopin, but according to what's happening here, in this room, and what is said here. Even if you were a nation so modestly endowed in greatness that your greatest artist were Tetmajer or Konopnicka; even then, if you knew how to speak of them with the naturalness of people who are mentally free, with the restraint and sobriety of mature people, if your words embraced the horizon not of a backwater but of the world . . . in such a case even Tetmajer would give you the right to glory. But as it is, Chopin and Mickiewicz serve only to bring into relief your own littleness—since, with the naivety of children, you wave your polonaises in the face of weary foreigners exclusively to prop up your impaired sense of your own value, and to make yourself seem more important. You are the poor cousins of the world, seeking to impress yourselves and others."

Yes, yes, the foregoing passage contains the acrimony of my first encounter with Poles abroad, from those Parisian times. And by that time I also felt something that a long time afterward I expressed in the same diary as follows:

Besides, those gathered there were aware they were foolish—foolish because they were dealing with matters they had mastered neither intellectually nor emotionally; hence this respect, this eager submissiveness to clichés, this admiration for Art, this conventional, learned language, this lack of genuineness and candor. Things were recited there. But the gathering was marked by discomfort, artificiality, and falseness also because Poland was taking part in it, and Poles never know how to behave in the presence of Poland, it disconcerts them and makes them affected. It intimidates them to such a degree that nothing "comes out right" for them; it makes them convulsive. They want to help Poland, and have an excessive desire to exalt it. Note that toward God (in church) Poles behave naturally and correctly; toward Poland they become confused—this is something to which they've not yet grown accustomed.

It seems to me that it isn't hard to understand the point of this passage and the preceding one: It is merely that Poles should adore Poland in a less naive, less provincial way, a way that doesn't betray the feeling of inferiority that gnaws at them when they are abroad. In a word, I mean the dignity and even, to speak in Sienkiewiczian terms, the honor of Poles in their encounter with the world. But this was not how Prime Minister Cyrankiewicz understood it; in the speech he gave to inaugurate the Year of Copernicus he make a fuss about how I had brought shame on Copernicus. Narrow-minded prudery! You, immortal Egeria, in Poland, even for a Marxist!

Let us return to my Paris in that year of 1928. Once the Chinese, Hsu, asked if I wouldn't like to go with him to visit a certain professor, at whose home an international company used to gather. "I warn you, though," he said: "There'll be Poles there."

"So what?"

"You may find it irritating."

"Why?"

"You'll see."

And I did see. Irritating? Certainly! There were perhaps ten foreigners there, who were behaving with all propriety, and there were two Poles—a young married couple—who . . . Thirty years later, this was how I described them in my diary:

I recall a tea at the home of a certain foreigner, where an acquaintance of mine, a Pole, began to speak about Poland—and naturally, out came Mickiewicz and Kościuszko along with King Jan Sobieski and the Relief of Vienna. The other foreigners listened politely to this earnest exposition and learned that "Nietzsche and Dostoevski were of Polish origin" and that "we have two Nobel Prizes in Literature." It occurred to me that if someone were to boast in this way about themselves or their family, it would be a serious faux pas. It occurred to me that this rivalry with other nations for geniuses and heroes, for cultural accomplishments and trophies, is highly impolitic from the point of view of propa-

ganda tactics—for in this we cannot withstand the competition from Italy, France, or England, and this very approach condemns us to being second-rate. The foreigners, however, continued to listen patiently, with forbearance, cordiality even; after all, they understood the situation du pauvre polonais, the poor Pole. The latter, intent on his role, went on and on. . . .

This description faithfully captures my torments during that visit with Hsu—I was already developing an antipathy toward that indefatigable, importunate "propaganda" of ours, and the patriotic urge to continually "advertise" Poland abroad. But in those Parisian years, I was not yet able to formulate a clear position on the nation; this happened only after the last war, when I set about writing *Trans-Atlantic*. Nevertheless, Paris in 1928 very much helped to intensify the attitude I took toward the nation. At that time I saw it from the outside. From abroad. This was a very instructive experience.

*

One day, walking down some Parisian street ("some" street, because I wasn't interested in the names of streets), I went into a church to take shelter from the rain.

To my surprise I saw something like a well, with a catafalque at the bottom. I stared at it and then left, because the rain had stopped.

Years later I found out that this was the tomb of Napoleon.

You must admit that for a future artist and so-called intellectual, this was a considerable, even scandalous dose of ignorance. It was worse still with the Louvre. One of my new friends was a lad with a very refined sense of artistic culture. He wrote poetry and moved in literary circles; he knew Gide well and even used to go and visit him in Cuverville. It was not clear to what he owed this honor—his Catholicism, his literary talents, or his peaches-and-cream complexion—for Gide was as many-sided as he was full of surprises. Once my friend brought a few writers to our little café, including Du Bos and Valéry Larbaud. But we didn't know Gide personally and so we could not know to what extent our Jules was just one more work by the great author—everything in him, from his manner and his views to his interests and his language, were taken from Gide. We were convinced, however, that he shone with his own light, not a borrowed one, and we were full of admiration for his brilliance.

Before long I became the chief object of his concern. He couldn't tolerate my indifference to art, thought, culture; like Gide, he was earnestly enthusiastic about matters of the mind, and he never missed any notable concert or important exhibition. In me he sensed material for an artist, and this was precisely what bothered him. He demanded that I take part in the whole worship; he wouldn't accept that I could not like poetry, painting, or music, and he asserted that I *must* like them! He accused me of pretense, of being mannered, of assuming a pose.

Once we went to the circus, and the antics of the two clowns amused us greatly.

"Why don't you bring Gide here so he can have a bit of a rest from his masterpieces?" I asked.

"Actually I wouldn't mind doing that," he replied, "but I'd be afraid he would burst into tears."

"Why? Tears of laughter, maybe."

"No. He always cries when he likes something very much. He'll shed buckets of tears at the best comedy, for the very reason that it's good and funny."

This seemed grotesque to me, and I began making fun of Gide—not for the first time either. Jules took offense. Later we had a sharp exchange of opinions and finally a serious talk in which he revealed how pained and shocked he was by my—in his view—artificial dislike of art and what he called my mania for camouflage. Jules's torments partly amused me and partly touched me—it was all very French, very Parisian, devoid of the modesty and discretion that my more northern temperament required. By way of an apology, I agreed to undertake with him a pilgrimage to the Louvre, which I'd not yet visited.

We went. The outing was a dramatic one.

At this time I was indeed ill-disposed toward art. I was filled with Schopenhauer and his opposition between life and contemplation, and also with Mann, in whom this contrast assumes an even more painful aspect. Art for me was the work of sickness, weakness, decadence. I did not like artists, I might say, "personally"; I preferred the world of action and people of action. These phobias had to be passionate at my age—twenty-something, when one hasn't yet given up on beauty. The artistic world attracted me with its freedom and glitter, but it repulsed me morally and physically.

Thus, the trip to the Louvre was far from innocent. Steps. Statues. Rooms. The moment we crossed the threshold of the sanctuary, something strange began to happen to us, though differently for each of us. He became reverent and trod on tiptoe, as if given wings by a sudden sharpening of his sensitivities; he was rapt as he walked up to the paintings, and it was obviously an intense experience for him. And it was precisely this that infuriated me, because I suspected his experience was for me, addressed to me, in an attempt to draw me into his adoration. And so the more he was exalted, the more I became phlegmatic and ill-disposed. With a supremely rustic mien I wandered through the galleries, which were filled with the boundless monotony of works of art; I breathed in that museum smell, which gives one a headache, and my gaze strayed from picture to picture with the combination of tedium and disdain that is engendered by excess. There was too much of it all—these masterpieces—and quantity overcame quality. And also that monotonous display, on those walls. I yawned.

Jules's face was close to hysteria and hatred.

"I'm bored," I said. "Let's go."

We went out into God's world. What delight: sunshine, women! He attacked me furiously; he was deeply upset. I shall pass over the quarrel that developed, but I'll cite the following excerpt from our dialogue, which was important for me:

"Why are you mad at me?" I asked. "I hope you realize that it wasn't the pictures I was looking at but something else."

"What?"

"The people. You look at pictures; I look at the people admiring the pictures. The admirers have stupid expressions, you understand? A person admiring a picture has a stupid face. It's a fact."

"Why?!"

This question took me by surprise—I didn't know why. Nevertheless, I was overcome by a sweet certainty that my observation was correct, and even in some way important: In that admiration there was definitely something stupid. I restricted myself to this reply:

"Why? Why? Don't you worry, if I think about it I'll figure out why. I'll telephone you when it comes to me."

Poor fellow! To this day he's waiting for my telephonic explanation; a long time had to pass before I was able to provide a more solid basis and justification for that war of mine with the fine arts, which began at that time in Paris, outside the Louvre. It was only after the war, in Argentina, that my hostile attitude toward painting began to crystallize. And my first public statement on this subject, an article in the Argentinian newspaper *La Nación,* in 1943 I believe, was entitled "Our Face and Mona Lisa's Face," and it concerned my Parisian experiences.

"The face of Mona Lisa—how beautiful it is!" I wrote in the article. "But what of it for us? It's beautiful, but it renders the faces of its devotees hideous. In the picture is beauty; in front of the picture is snobbery, stupidity, a dull-witted effort to grasp something of the beauty about which one is told that it exists."

Today I see the extent to which my reactions were Polish—they belonged to the Polish gentry, the Polish countryside; they were Polish through and through. That incurable Polishness of mine, with which I'm afflicted at every step abroad, almost makes me laugh—to find it in a person like me supposedly "liberated" from every bond. The Polish distrust of art, especially the fine arts, is in my blood.

Once I was shouted at in the little café where we gathered for discussions.

"Poles like pictures too! It's just that they have to have them brought from abroad. Painters as well, because you don't have your own. And you weren't even capable of recognizing their talent and respecting them."

I replied as follows: "We have a saying: 'The nose isn't for the snuff-box but the snuff-box for the nose.' Likewise, people are not for painting; painting is for people. Painting should be treated from a position of superiority, instead of falling on one's knees in front of the pictures."

I didn't realize at the time that I was uttering one of the most important formulas of my entire subsequent development.

*

I gradually came to feel comfortable in Paris, and eventually I might well have turned into a Parisian, but complications arose. I did no studying whatsoever, took no exams, and did not show my face at the Graduate Institute for International Studies; how could I explain this to my father, who in his letters asked about my progress? Luckily, those partially cured "upper" lungs reappeared, and I got a slight fever with an accompanying exhaustion. Janek Baliński took care of me and sent me to a doctor. Realizing that this illness was a gift from heaven, the best possible excuse for my idleness, I put on a show of suffering for the physician, who determined that I ought to leave immediately for the mountains in the south.

In this way, one night I found myself on a train bound for the *département* of Pyrénées Orientales, a stone's throw from Spain, where the Pyrenees descend to the Mediterranean. As I traveled my mind was pulsating, in a state of ferment produced by my stay in Paris, and it was on that night it became clear to me I would be an artist—a writer. As I plunged into the night I had the impression that I was plunging into my own future. Nothing special happened to me on that journey (in general nothing ever happens to me), and yet even today, when I'm on a train at night, and mysterious lights and inscrutable shapes flash by outside the window, I'm reminded powerfully of that journey filled to the brim with presentiments so strong they almost seemed real.

Yet it isn't true that nothing unusual happened. In fact something did. In my compartment there was a young and rather unattractive Scottish woman; I got talking to her and passed a good part of the night in conversation. I no longer remember the route the train took, but it turned out that our paths would diverge, in Perpignan I think. At this discovery my Scottish woman gave a cry of delight that at last she'd found someone in whom she could confide—someone with whom she found it easy to converse and whom she would never see again; for she was going to take a short vacation by the sea and then would return to Scotland, where I certainly wouldn't go—and straight away she began to share the details of her confidences, which were indeed awful, since in her family things far from decent had taken place, and my Scottish woman had taken an active part in them. We parted warmly in Perpignan. But that wasn't the end of this strange story.

Around midday I arrived at my destination: Le Boulou, a small spa in the Pyrenees. Most of the next day was spent playing billiards with the locals, working-class folk who traveled almost exclusively by bicycle and who were so adept at billiards I was barely able to demonstrate that Poles also know how to act on cue. But the closeness of the Mediterranean, which I had never set eyes on at that time, began to trouble me—that *thalassa* was nearby, less than thirty kilometers away, and the road led headlong downhill, for the mountains came to an end right at the sea—an inclined plane thanks to which a bicycle was promoted to the rank of motorcycle.

And so when I learned that on the coming Sunday my fellow billiard players were planning a trip to the beach at Banyuls, I rented a bicycle and in the early morning we set off in a large group along the downhill highway.

It was a marvelous excursion, filled with a poetry hard to convey, because it was composed of insignificant details and soaked in sunshine. My companions were no older than I was—young working people, garrulous, animated, good-humored in the French way and very entertaining. We fortified ourselves with oranges, bananas, and wine, and so the descent to Banyuls involved ever more bizarre zigzags, and in the end I was so sozzled that when we reached our destination, I couldn't for the life of me remember how to dismount from a bicycle and I kept riding round and round the square, desperately trying to figure out how to make the bicycle stop so I could get off it.

But I remember how, as I was riding along with that group of riotous southerners, for the first time in the distance the still and lustrous sheet of water of the Latino- [one line missing in the typescript] appeared to me all of a sudden, as if a curtain had been raised. That which all the cathedrals and museums of Paris had been unable to achieve was managed by the ribbon of that vertiginous highway heading straight for the sea, and all at once I understood the South, France, Italy, Rome, and a thousand other things. Everything for the first time became precious to me—me, who until then had regarded dark-haired people as an inferior species. The white of the stones, the noble grayness of the plane trees, the azure in front of us and above us, the distinctness of lines, the plenitude of the shapes—I understood it all. And I was enraptured, and that sacred feeling came over me as I was hurtling along like a madman amidst a group of drunken and vociferous workers whose uncouthness melded easily and spontaneously with their culture. The whole of French culture, which till that point had been bourgeois and repulsive to me, now appeared as something elemental and almost savage—I was won over. And from that moment I was no longer repulsed by the South.

Banyuls consists of a tiny harbor and a few cottages tucked into colorful nooks in the rugged coast. It's charming, though mawkish, sugary-sweet, postcard-pretty—I dislike the kind of beauty that is too much for show. Yet the purity of the contours, the immaculate severity of the play of light and shade, the white of the flat-roofed houses, and the festive blueness were sublime and reconciled me to the landscape. I decided to stay there, though it wasn't what had been ordered by my doctor, who had recommended the mountains. The next day I dragged my suitcase down the hill and found a guesthouse. Alas, an overpowering heat poured down from the sky, and then there came a huge storm, one of the greatest that had ever struck those shores. There was no rain—only a wind that raged with such intensity that everything seemed utterly blown through, as if intoxicated on wind, exhausted. It howled and blustered even in closed rooms. And towering waves of which I would never have thought the Mediterranean capable crashed thunderously against the wretched, drenched, moaning beach.

It lasted for three days. The fourth day brought reprieve, sweetness and joy; birds sang, while I was in a capital mood and was strolling along the beach in the company of some young ladies from my guesthouse when suddenly—ha! It was my Scottish woman, the one from the train! Twenty yards away, sitting on the sand! Upon seeing me she flushed a deep crimson; I, unfortunately, blush easily and at the sight of her embarrassment I myself turned red as a beetroot. And one of the girls who was with me noticed and commented with a touch of malice, "I see you two know each other!"

There was nothing for it; in Banyuls everyone knew one another, and so even if we hadn't been betrayed by our blushes it would have been hard to avoid an encounter. That same evening we both took part in a walk along the cliffs, and during the day the beach constantly brought us together. Of course it was much more discomfiting for her than for me. The poor woman: When I told her in the train that I was headed for the mountains, she was certain she'd never see me again, since she was going to the seaside; but we were both forgetting that here the mountains and the sea are right next to each other. The worst part, though, was that she kept turning bright scarlet, which in turn made me flush—at the slightest word that could be taken as an allusion to our earlier conversation we would both be overcome by blushes.

After two days I'd had enough and decided to leave Banyuls. I took all my belongings and moved to nearby Vernet-les-Bains, a town more picturesque than Le Boulou. Very good. I don't ask anyone to believe me: The next morning, leaving my hotel I turned a profound shade of red while in front of me there burst out another attack of blushes—it was her, the Scottish woman, all vermillion as she was getting off a bus with her cases.

She had also hit on the idea of leaving Banyuls and moving to Vernet!

A few times in life I've experienced so-called coincidences that were so astonishing I would never dare include anything like that in a novel. It's rather like those sunsets of which it is said, "If someone had painted it people would say it was over the top."

*

September 12, 1960

Summer was coming. I returned to Poland for the vacation, and that was the end of my Parisian studies, which, truth be told, had never started—I don't know if I visited that Institute of International Studies of mine more than a couple of times during my entire stay. Despite this, however, my encounter with the West was immensely important both in sharpening my Polish distinctness and bringing me into Europe.

It seems to me that in these recollections, as I describe my own problems I'm at bottom describing the formation of a Pole of my generation, and that is perhaps more important to me than telling anecdotes from my own life.

Poland seen after a lengthy stay abroad proved to be no less instructive than Paris. For the first time I was able to see through new eyes things amongst which I had grown up and which for this reason had never before attracted my attention. One disagreeable memory will forever remain with me—I don't know why this one and not another. The day after I returned from Paris I got into a Warsaw tram. The faces. Faces that were somnolent, torpid, flaccid, haggard . . . the poverty that is as overpowering as sleep . . . and that Slavic ponderousness. And that strange, exotic clothing, no longer European. For a long time after Paris I was on the lookout for un-Europeanness in Poland; I tried to discover the essence of Poland's marginality in relation to Europe.

What was most noticeable was the proletariat. The people!

I began to understand: In the West there was no proletariat, at least in the Polish sense of the word. There were intellectual workers and physical workers, richer people and poorer people; but in most cases indigence was not so heightened as to create a separate category of people, another "class." Barefooted girls on the streets of Paris were unthinkable.

But all the ferment that I brought from Paris I assiduously concealed from my family and acquaintances. It was important to me that people shouldn't say Paris had changed me—it seemed to me to be in the worst possible taste to be one of those young people who return from the West civilized. I behaved exactly as I had before; I dismissed Paris and France with quips and witticisms, and above all I never confessed to my ever growing attachment to Europe and to the spirit of Europe. True, this Europeanness of mine in no way interfered with my being in Poland or caused me to want to leave once again. I was too lazy, and, let's be honest, life in the bosom of my family was much more pleasant than wandering from hotel to hotel. So I didn't press my parents, who for their part had no illusions regarding my alleged studies at the Institute. "Even the Parisians can't make a silk purse out of a sow's ear," my father would say ironically when he was asked about my progress. I gave up the idea of further studies in Paris and took a position as a legal intern with an investigating magistrate by the name of Myszkorowski.

It was interesting work. The investigating magistrates had their offices in a building on Nowy Zjazd, overlooking the Vistula. My supervisor, Judge Myszkorowski, had two small rooms which one entered from a long hallway filled with prisoners and police officers. The first room contained the desks of us three interns; the second was occupied by the judge.

Our task was to prepare criminal cases that had been referred to the district court—in other words, the more serious ones. The judge would pass me the files from the preliminary investigation conducted by the police.

"Mr. Gombrowicz, a curious little case—I'm giving it to you because I know you like playing chess. Here's the problem: Did he forge it or didn't he? Questions need to be asked about all the various circumstances; and you need to take a close look at the investigation."

The files contained reports by police officers, cross-questionings that the police had carried out "on the fly," autopsies, and so on. Everything had to be read carefully, and the police inquiry had to be conducted over again, to make it more thorough and give it a legal form. Of course, the judge himself was in charge of the whole thing and signed all the papers, but he left us room for maneuver. And when the terrified wrongdoer, escorted by a police officer, sat on the little chair in front of my desk I felt rather proud, especially because we had instructions not to disabuse the accused and the witnesses when they called us "your honor." "It's always better that he should think he's testifying in front of a judge than in front of an intern," our superior would say about this order.

During more than a year spent with these investigations I came into contact with the dregs of society in various manifestations: murders, political crimes, sex crimes, theft, fraud. We occasionally had to deal with the insane; sometimes we were obliged to be present at autopsies, which was not the most agreeable part of the job. I remember that the first time this happened was on my birthday. I ate a light breakfast, aware that it might not stay in my stomach for very long, after which I went to a dingy building in which a doctor in a white apron was diligently sawing through the skull of some unfortunate late lamented. Our role as interns was much harder than that of the doctors—above all, they were accustomed to it, and besides, they were engrossed in their work, whereas we were not only novices but, having nothing to occupy ourselves with, we were condemned to look on, prey to all kinds of caprices of the imagination.

It might be thought that I learned some useful lessons from this contact with destitution and vice; however, quite the opposite was the case. I've long noted that there is nothing a person grows accustomed to faster than precisely these "lower depths" of existence; the process is even quicker if one's contact is of a professional nature, as a doctor, for instance, or a legal intern. After a few months I had entered an administrative routine; these people were "processed" and that was the end of it. I retained only one quality with which I was probably born, yet which is not exactly desirable in a judge: a complete failure to comprehend that the person I was badgering with insidious questions was actually "guilty." I was much closer to the point of view of the criminal, who had "gotten into trouble" through bad luck. This certitude regarding a person's absolute innocence was not some deterministic philosophy of mine, but a spontaneous feeling that I couldn't suppress.

This sometimes created curious situations. Once, in the district court—at the time I was assigned to this court, where I served as recorder—after ordering a recess, the presiding judge ordered me to ask the accused some question. Walking up to the dock, I calmly shook the criminal's hand, and it was only the astonished stares of the lawyers that made me realize my indiscretion.

The work of recording the sessions wasn't so easy. A session would begin at nine in the morning and often go on into the night, with only a short meal break in the afternoon. During those many hours

one had constantly to pay attention. The cases were often complicated and entirely unfamiliar to the wretched recorder; you had to
grasp them as you went along. And how often they were submerged
in the gibberish spouted by terrified simpletons, hysterical women,
or professional conmen! At times the presiding judge was muddle-
headed and introduced the most fearful confusion into the matter.
Worst of all were the judges who had an elevated opinion of their
own mental acuity and liked to show off—a judge of this sort would
interrupt the person testifying in mid-sentence in order to move on
to the next point, and the job of correctly formulating the response
in the record was left to the recorder.

Fortunately, sessions were only held twice a week. After the sitting
I would take the files home, prepare a clean version of the record, and
then I'd be free till the next session.

Once the secretary of the court came up to me. He said, "The
judges have asked for you to prepare the applications for text changes
in the printed forms."

"Why me in particular?"

"You're considered the best of the interns."

Me? I was most surprised. I had been unaware of this. Even more
interestingly, I made no effort whatsoever to find out if it was true. I
already sensed I was not going to be a lawyer.

*

My job in the court didn't take up much of my time—no more
than two days a week in all. I filled the rest of the week with books,
of which I consumed a great number at random (the method, or
rather lack of method, most likely to lead to intellectual growth, as I
became convinced in later life). But I also returned to my other occupation, which I'd long since abandoned: writing.

This time, however, these were not compositions abortive right
from their botched conception; I engaged in level-headed work aimed
at a concrete result. I set about writing brief pieces—short stories—
with the idea that if one didn't work out I would burn it and start

something new. But all of them came out well, in my view at least. During those university years, when on the surface I had distanced myself entirely from literature, a style was forming within me, and now from the first moment I discovered in myself a sureness of hand that I could never have anticipated.

My thoughts often return to those first literary works of mine, which, as it turns out today, were not at all so trivial—quite the opposite, they've found some notable admirers around the world. I strive to recall the extent to which I was aware of what I was doing. For example, did I realize how modern that prose was? How different it was in spirit and form from our literature at that time?

But it's extremely difficult for me today to recreate my state of mind then, the more so because writing is laborious, meticulous work, a daily struggle with the text one is engaged on, and because in addition I was writing somewhat blindly, paying no attention to the general character of my questionable "creativity." One thing I do remember—that from the beginning the nonsensical and the absurd were very much to my liking, and I was never more satisfied than when my pen gave birth to some scene that was truly crazy, removed from the (healthy) expectations of mediocre logic, and yet firmly rooted in its own separate logic.

This was how I came to write the stories "The Lawyer Kraykowski," "The Memoirs of Stefan Czarniecki," "Crime with Premeditation" and "Virginity." I showed them to no one. I was embarrassed. Despite living in Warsaw, and my work as an intern, I was still someone "from the country," a true scion of my sphere of the landed gentry. And though by now I was thoroughly familiar with all the naivety and indolence of those bumpkins, something of their mistrust of art and artists had permanently attached itself to me. Literary work seemed a little ridiculous. To be an artist, to be a poet—how gauche! Furthermore, the actions of a young man preparing his first lucubrations were doomed to be incurably pretentious.

One thing was certain, and of this I was aware: that my attempts at writing were in sharp opposition—opposition to everything—their tone was one of rebellion. "If I enter that House of Lords," I thought to myself, "like Lord Byron, it'll be to sit on the side of the opposition."

At the same time I was consumed by another passion: tennis. I joined the Legia sports club and soaked it all in—that is, the club atmosphere, the rivalry, the hierarchies that formed amongst the players; for me, all this made tennis infinitely more meaningful than my previous amateur appearances on various "courts" in the country. I began to play with great enthusiasm, and I made some progress, though I never became an outstanding player.

As you can see, my life at this time was still immeasurably frivolous. It was a privileged life, remote from real life—it was perhaps only the daily toil over my short stories that smacked of true exertion. At the same time I was prey to moments of intense despair and utter mortification. Was this life? Would I continue to be a parasite, entertaining myself with stories, tennis, and my legal internship, which was also not really work but only a simulacrum of work? A dull rage at everything that filled my existence with privilege—money, provenance, education, connections, everything that made me a sybarite and an idler, that rose between me and life like a glass screen—gnawed at me more and more, and I very nearly became a communist. I was never so close to communism as at that time; I was embittered, empty, furious at myself. I would have loved to use communism as a tool to smash the complex of conditions that defined me so fatefully. But I could never rid myself of the conviction that communism is a theory incapable of transforming life; those intellectual schemas seemed inapplicable in practice.

Then, in Zakopane once, a simple truth about my life came to me, and this truth was a true privilege for me.

I'm expressing myself poetically, because it was poetry. It happened one evening in the Kościelisko Valley. I was alone and tired as

I walked along—my two companions had gone missing somewhere along the way. I was walking and once again I was visited by the distressing awareness that I was wasting time, that I was not living, that I was going to waste. The mountains above me were less oppressive than these accursed thoughts of mine. Then before me I noticed a hostel, a handsome Zakopane chalet from which a handsome young woman emerged, a waitress. I asked for something to eat. The waitress sat down at my table; I shared my beer with her. There was no one around; the highland silence, the freshness of the mountains, the freshness of this girl; without a second thought I poured out all the torments that until then I'd kept hidden from the world, just like the Scottish woman who confided in me in France, because she thought she would never see me again. The girl was at ease; she clearly had the ease produced by a sporting lifestyle, but she was pure too with the purity that also comes from sport. She listened to me carefully.

"There's nothing to it!" she decreed. "Of course you have an easy life—but for you, your easy life is harder than for another person their difficult life, so it amounts to the same thing!"

This truth wouldn't have dazzled me as much as it did had it not come from this woman, who was the embodiment of health and simplicity. Someone called upon as a woman to pass judgment on men. That was right! I didn't have an easy life! I had a difficult life, because my life's very easiness was difficult for me.

I was beginning to understand my calling, and this helped to set my mind at rest. I don't wish to weigh these recollections down with overly subtle reasoning. I'll just say in broad terms that I had discovered a strategy widely used in art—transforming weakness into strength, and defects into values. If I was not sufficiently authentic or connected with reality, then it was precisely this that could become my authentic and real drama.

But for the meantime, I continued to devote myself to the construction of fanciful stories, putting off till later the accounts I had to settle with life—my own and others'. I was engrossed in developing a form for myself, discovering my own properties as a stylist and a storyteller . . . Imagination! I let it gambol where it would; following in its wake, I organized what it unearthed for me.

Other than Staś Baliński—whom I didn't entirely trust in such matters—I was not close to anyone from the literary world. Then, in 1928 I think it was, I went off to Zakopane again, this time for the winter, and took a room in the Mirabella guesthouse, which was owned by Canoness Szczuka, a friend of my sister's. It was a small boardinghouse run by the canoness herself. The moment I arrived I realized I was in trouble. Another friend of my sister's, Halina Dernałowicz, was staying there with her mother, and there were also other people from so-called society, which meant I had to be on my best behavior, especially because the ladies were very moral and Catholic.

But a few days later, when I was already seriously thinking about moving elsewhere, there appeared a tall, slightly stooping, dark-haired young man with a distinguished face and a twinkle in his eye, who was bursting with energy—Tadeusz Breza. I suspect that those who know Breza today (he is now a writer and, I believe, the cultural attaché at the Polish embassy in Rome) can have no idea what a fire-cracker he was in his youth.

*

I know few people for whom the occupation of writer seemed simultaneously so appropriate and so incongruous as it was for Tadeusz Breza. That is, it seemed appropriate in some regards, but it didn't give the slightest indication of his other personal qualities. Breza's writing is subtle, refined, scrupulous, perceptive, precise, devoted tenderly to its purpose. All this you will find in him at first glance when you read him. But where in this writing is Tadeusz's crazy sense of humor, his verve, his poetic drive—at least when I saw him then, in his youth, appearing before me at Halina Szczuka's guesthouse in Zakopane?

Sprawling on the sofa amongst those young ladies who have remained in my memory—Krysia Skarbek, Lizia Krasicka, the Tabęcka sisters, the canoness, who was awfully young herself, the Chodkiewicz girls—with his aura of a habitué of literary circles, an acquaintance of the Skamandrists, a friend of Iwaszkiewicz, he made himself the center of the conversation, which soon became a mad dance of absurdities. "You're not really any good for anything," Tadeusz would explain to one of them. "It's not clear what you should be used for. I suppose at a pinch you could be employed for carrying heavy weights, but it would be better just to use you as a weight yourself, as ballast; yes, we could tie you to the end of a rope for when furniture's being hoisted to an upper floor. Though I'm not so sure, because you're from the country, so perhaps you ought to be planted, like a radish. Or maybe it'd be better to use you as ground for planting; we could grow radishes in your ears." The nonsense would multiply, embracing ever broader, more unexpected topics. I found this kind of humor entrancing.

This genre of Tadeusz's allowed him to do things whose boldness took one's breath away. For example, out of the blue he would start to use familiar language with the older ladies. He would go up to the sofa on which the aged Mrs. Chodkiewicz reigned in her majesty, and he would say at the top of his voice, "Hey, Mrs. C., how's you today? What're you up to?" Strange to relate, the elderly women forgave him. He was unflagging in thinking up new practical jokes; once, just for fun he stole some silverware at a reception.

I immediately made friends with Tadeusz, but our friendship was complicated from the start. He found it hard to grasp all my various sore points and complexes, which prevented me from feeling relaxed. He couldn't understand how I could combine such an extensive knowledge of culture with a complete lack of social know-how; nor did he notice that the presence of my sister's friends made me so very ill at ease—not because I cared so much what they thought of me, but because I couldn't find the right form to use with them. I was irritated by Tadeusz's excessive subtleties, his inordinate delicacy. Despite this, in Warsaw we became even closer, and I joined his circle: Kasia Turno, who at that time I believe was his fiancée, the Mauersbergers, Tonio Sobański, Jerzy Paczkowski, subsequently the editor of *Szpilki,* and several others. Adaś Mauersberger and his sister, Zosia, brought a great deal of liveliness to those meetings, and their parents' home on Senatorska soon became our second gathering place.

Eventually I showed Tadeusz my stories—four of them—and asked him what he thought. He returned them with expressions of enthusiastic praise; in his view they were of considerable value. And to prove to me he really wasn't joking, he took me to breakfast with Grydzewski, the editor of *Wiadomości Literackie,* and Jarosław Iwaszkiewicz.

I went, not without anxiety and curiosity. Iwaszkiewicz was already famous despite the fact that he was still young; the Skamandrists were already renowned for being new and out of the ordinary, and Grydzewski's *Wiadomości Literackie* constituted the center of this cultural revolution, which along with the other revolutions of the postwar period was transforming tastes and customs. Up till now I'd had no contact with these stars; our circle, mine and Tadeusz's, was second class. We went to a restaurant on the Plac Teatralny, the name of which I don't remember. What I do remember is that that first encounter with the *Wiadomości* group left an unpleasant taste in my mouth. Today Iwaszkiewicz and I are friends, and I cannot forget that he was the first reader of my play *The Marriage* and that his enthusiastic response gave me strength at a time when I'd almost completely gone to seed in my Argentinian seclusion. But that's one thing; it's quite another matter that the breakfast was not a great success.

Grydzewski consumed with relish vast quantities of cold cuts. The conversation was confined to sayings and clever little witticisms, but even these weren't especially sharp, which was no doubt in part my fault—because once again, as if out of spite, in the presence of these literati I assumed the style of a bumpkin, a rustic, which had already gotten me into so much trouble in Paris.

"What are those scraps of paper?" Iwaszkiewicz asked Tadeusz in a most dismissive way, indicating some papers that lay on the table.

"Oh, nothing," replied Breza in embarrassment. "They're mine." These were the typescripts of my stories, which he'd brought in order to show them to Iwaszkiewicz. Had Jarosław guessed that they were my texts, and in this way was giving us to understand that after meeting me in person he harbored no illusions regarding them? Or perhaps it was entirely unintentional? In any case this incident thoroughly dampened my enthusiasm, and for a long time stopped me from wanting to be closer to the Skamandrists.

I was very proud. I couldn't bear the fact that these already successful men had treated me condescendingly. I wouldn't accept a second-rank or third-rank role, but as yet I had no claim to glory. They too had no reason to take me seriously, since my pride prevented me from seeking their approval, and it was precisely with them, as if by design, that I behaved much worse than with others.

Skamander! Those fellows were born under a lucky star. They entered literature at a moment when warm, invigorating winds were blowing in Europe, windows were opening, and prison walls were crumbling. They breathed the air of revolution, yet not the brutal kind, but the mild sort conducive to art. They began writing poems at a time when the world needed poetry and was looking for it. They constituted an exceptionally well-matched and closely knit group. They found an excellent impresario in editor Grydzewski. They immediately gained popularity, influence, even fame. Yes indeed . . . It's just that such conditions give rise to major or minor talents, but not to true literature—this requires precisely an atmosphere that is less propitious, less, I might say, social. It grows on the side, in isolation, in opposition, in timidity and shame, rebellion and anxiety. In this sense my peers and I were in a more fortunate position—we faced a path that was harder and more fertile. I don't know when I first became aware of the intellectual and artistic bankruptcy of the Skamandrists, but long before the war I no longer had any illusions: Nothing could be expected of them beyond the regular supply of better or worse poems. They weren't the kind who discover new lands in art, enrich our knowledge of humankind, create a new style, or introduce new kinds of disquiet. Some of them, like Tuwim, Iwaszkiewicz, or Słonimski, achieved lofty positions in Polish poetry or prose, but not in Polish creativity.

They didn't lack for shrewdness or tactical adroitness. Later on I'll recount how they terrorized a Warsaw café, and along with it the press too; without being creative artists on a grander scale they nevertheless developed their own genre, and that guaranteed them the upper hand until the war swept everything away.

*

As I slowly began to be part of the community of artists, my legal internship progressed, though rather sluggishly. I worked in the regional court and the appellate court, always as a secretary, whose duties involved making a formal record of the hearings. This work suited me: It left me sufficient time for literature, and I even grew so proficient at keeping the record that during the hearing itself, at less intense moments I was able to scribble something literary on the side.

The court became a kind of opening through which I entered into the wretchedness of life in general and Polish life in particular. This wasn't new to me—I knew it well, not so much from my own experience as from the fact that I was very sensitive to it and I didn't yield to illusions, something that means more than any advantage coming from personal encounters with wretchedness. But in the court this acquired form for me; the court was like a perpetual theater showing me the drama of the lower world in its various shapes. I watched from my seat by the judge's desk; at times I was close to bursting out in malicious and bitter applause.

I also observed the upper spheres called upon to pass judgment on the lower ones—the judges, prosecutors, lawyers. I liked the judges infinitely more than the lawyers, whom I found repugnant—as I do to this day—for their pretentiousness, their rhetoric, their oratorical maneuvers, for all their legal talk, which strains toward culture, humanism, and philosophy, while at root they're usually far from any kind of mastery of these domains. In court it became clear that their studies of the law had given them neither the general education of which they were so proud, nor good manners in the deeper, humanistic sense of the phrase. And their confrontation with human misery left much to be desired.

Despite all that's been written and said about me for many years, I was never indifferent to the dismal matter of the easy life of the rich and the hard life of the poor; on the contrary, this matter caused me a great deal of pain and suffering ever since my earliest childhood. It's just that . . . But I should rather cite a dialogue with one of the writers with communist sympathies whom I had recently met—was it not Ważyk? I no longer remember who it was, nor in which year exactly this conversation took place; but for me it was a rather significant one.

It began when he made some dismissive reference to my sybaritism and my "innocence." He said something along the lines of, "What's the point of talking to you? You don't know life; you live as if in a hothouse, far away from the struggle for existence. What can you know about such social problems?"

This was my Achilles heel—but I now knew how to defend myself. I didn't immediately respond, but later in the conversation I returned seemingly by chance to this topic and began to speak of what I had seen in court, about the dramas I'd observed. But I tried to show in both the tone and the substance of what I said that I wasn't so unfamiliar with this reality.

He looked at me in surprise.

"Here I was thinking you were a milksop, but I see that you really know a thing or two about all this."

I replied, "I'm familiar with life and I know what it is better than you communists, even though I've never experienced poverty."

It sounded arrogant, but it may not have been so far from the truth: Personal experience of something doesn't always increase one's sensitivity, and sometimes, on the contrary, diminishes it.

"If you're so keenly aware of these things," he said, "why don't you become a communist?"

"Not because I don't agree with your goals," I replied, "but because I don't believe that you'll succeed in achieving anything. You'll just make an even bigger mess."

These words depicted my sense of powerlessness in the face of the so-called social question. I didn't believe it could be resolved by revolution, five-year plans, a system, a scheme. I was convinced that theories, dreams, and upheavals can only delay the slow, organic work in all fields—scientific, technical, moral—that is the only way of improving the lot of the proletariat. There always seemed to be something amiss with the people of revolution and of communism whom I encountered. They were either dreamers, or people of envy, or theoreticians; and I didn't think them capable of practical accomplishments. I believed that such huge problems couldn't be solved by moral reasoning, nor by the most splendid idealism; and that what was needed above all was something called efficacy. For this reason I never attempted to introduce into my emerging art any of the rebellious feelings that I experienced in court; this would be inefficacious and impractical, from the point of view both of life and of art.

Something else, however, could bring certain results. Something else could be done—by me, as a writer and an artist. And that something also revealed itself to me during the court hearings.

What can this something be called? I wasn't able to contribute to the improvement of the lot of the lower spheres; but who knew if I couldn't contribute to an improvement in the behavior of the upper spheres toward the lower—of the intelligentsia passing judgment on the proletariat, or on the semi-intelligent.

Do you recall how irritated I was by the landed gentry, the corpulent, loud-mouthed landowners, compared with the common people—these distorted people compared with straightforward people? Their arrogance, their gracelessness, naivety, gluttony, their bellies, their pamperedness, their sicknesses? All this had a common cause—the privileged life that money makes possible. The same thing that I myself was troubled by! Well then: The representatives of the upper social classes with whom I had to deal in court, those functionaries of justice, were much more deserving of respect. They worked, often very hard, they knew the meaning of responsibility and discipline, and they sometimes even experienced mortifications—thanks to which, without embarrassment they could look those they were passing judgment on and sentencing in the eye. And yet my sensitivity, attuned in this regard, whispered in my ear that something here was awry—I sensed something false in the way those people behaved. Their superiority was too sure of itself. Too supercilious. It looked as if they felt themselves called to control, to train the proletariat—and nothing more. Yet those judges and lawyers, though they were better than the landed gentry, were also far from perfection themselves; those bald pates in their pince-nez, those soft, plump intellectual bodies looked rather unconvincing, and it was hard to resist the impression that they were also a caricature, but an upside-down one. If a life of poverty deformed the proletariat, if comfort and inactivity deformed the landowners, then the urban intelligentsia was also misshapen by its lifestyle. So does life never produce a full person? Did there always have to be such mutually complementary fragments of humanity?

What angered me in the judges and lawyers was that, intent on their role and intoxicated by their function, they forgot about their own unsightliness and imperfection. They knew only their own superiority and the violence that the law put in their hands. They forgot their own nakedness—both the physical and the intellectual. They were incapable of seeing themselves from the outside, and this was an error of style, an error of form of immense significance, since it made people no more than the product of their class, their social group, cut them off from other lives, constricted them, limited them, rendered any creative contact with other categories of humans impossible. So many lives to which they had no access! And neither did I!

To destroy this form of theirs and impose another that would permit the upper classes to draw closer to the lower, to enter into a creative relation with them . . . Yes! But how could this be achieved?

*

October 27, 1960

In the meantime Warsaw's appearance was changing. Its stone pavements, the famous cobblestones, were disappearing, as were horse-drawn cabs, gaiters, walking sticks, bowler hats, top hats, patent leather shoes, stiff shirtfronts, and stiffness in general. The difference in age of ten years between my oldest brother and me was enough to reveal vividly the accelerated tempo of these changes. My brother was one of the "golden youth" already on its way out. He was, as the phrase went, "from the country"; he made a show, waved a cane as he walked, and stared at women like a ladies' man. In the theater he was only ever seen in the front rows, and in everything he maintained the ways of the landed gentry. I, on the other hand, did not carry a cane, had to force myself to wear a wing collar, did not frequent fashionable restaurants, did not have affairs of honor, and did not "go on the prowl" or spend my time carousing. My brother, however strapped for cash he was, always pulled up in front of Lourse's café in a stylish horse-drawn cab, which, when he was truly down on his luck, he would hire at a nearby corner simply so that he could arrive at Lourse's with the necessary flourish. I—to the considerable mortification of my family and various relatives amongst the gentry—often got around by bicycle when I was in the country, and in town I traveled almost exclusively by tram.

My father welcomed these changes, merely complaining from

time to time that along with the anachronisms the former decency not just of manners but of minds was disappearing. Yet some of the antics of us young folk got under his skin.

I remember that once he and I went to visit my grandmother, my mother's mother, who lived in Bodzechów in a detached house, which incidentally was a rather terrifying place, since in the night-time it was filled with wild, fearful singing that turned into shouts, rasping, whimpering, frantic relentless dialogues, mournful whispers, and bitter weeping. No, it was not ghosts. Her son, who had gone insane at the age of twenty, lived with her. The house was divided into two parts, in one of which the madman reigned; and since at night he was visited by fear in rooms where he had only his own solitude, he cheered himself with this concert, which was enough to chill the blood of anyone unaccustomed to it.

But let's return to our topic. When my father and I arrived in Bodzechów I discovered that my grandmother's new maid, Marysia, was very good-looking, and so on Sunday I invited her to a performance by the local amateur dramatic society. As chance would have it, that very Sunday some guests were supposed to come, and grandmother asked Marysia if she couldn't move her "free time" to another day. "I can't," answered Marysia, "because the young master's invited me to the theater." "Oh, my dear, if you and the young master are going to the theater together, of course that's an entirely different matter!" replied my grandmother, looking askance at my father. Such far-reaching democracy was too much for him, and after Marysia left he gave me a stern dressing-down. "This is demoralizing for the servants!" he said. I defended myself, saying that Marysia had the evening off and so for those few hours she wasn't a maid. "Besides," I said, "I really don't understand why I can't go to the theater with the maid—what's the harm in that?" But it was precisely this that my father couldn't understand—and it was hardly surprising! I was already an urbanite, in other words essentially democratic, accustomed to service that was anonymous, almost abstract; whereas he was from the times when one had personal servants with whom it was necessary to keep one's distance; being a master for him was still a virtue.

The generation I belonged to was in a situation rarely encountered by any Polish generation. We had grown up in a free and independent country, and this idyll was to last all of twenty years! Before my eyes this independence, at first somewhat hazy and ill-defined, acquired flesh and blood. But I can't say I was especially enthusiastic about it; my generation quickly grew accustomed to freedom, and the reemergence of an independent Polish state soon became the purely official topic of various formal speeches. How can the patriotism of my generation be described? That it was no longer romanticism is common knowledge; but it should be added that neither did it contain sentimentality or honor, that "honor" which was ever less popular and smacked ever more of comicality. Amongst us there arose a great embarrassment on the subject of our homeland, and it may well have been this that distinguished us so clearly from the young people of the time of Żeromski, with their fondness for brandishing flags and plumed headdresses. In this respect my friends were like me—it was harder and harder for them to produce patriotic effusions in prose or poetry; their sensitivity protected itself with cynicism, and they preferred making jokes to making speeches. Early military experiences, especially those in 1920, also probably contributed to such a sober disposition. At that time, not only had we entered independence without illusions and with a rather practical attitude, but also we entirely lacked a language in which to express our attachment to Poland, because the language we had inherited was already hopelessly out of date, and no one had taught us a newer, authentic way of speaking that was suited to our needs, our kind, and our style. In this sense we were utterly untamed—we were mute. And yet we were all thoroughly and indubitably Poles, which became apparent when this strange independence was once again submerged, first in Germany and then later in communism. I include myself in the nation, though I didn't risk my own neck and only observed these new occupations from far-off America—but the fact that, despite a long time spent abroad, I did not lose my nationality as a writer also means something, and testifies to the strength of my ties with the country of my birth.

But at the same time, in order to understand the curious, as it were concealed patriotism of my peers, it needs to be borne in mind that this generation was, generally speaking, in a certain sense "un-awoken"; or to put it another way, despite its characteristic matter-of-factness it was removed from reality. This shouldn't be particularly surprising, since the leap from 1914 to, say, 1920, was fearfully large: Changes occurred at a gallop, one after another, in every field. And this dulled our sensitivity, especially because we lived through that gallop as children. In all probability, our most important discovery was the fact that nothing special was happening and there was nothing in particular to worry about. Poland had suddenly burst into life? The dreams of prophets and nonprophets alike had turned into reality? So what? Poland existed and that was all there was to it. Einstein, Skamander, futurism, the liberation of women, surrealism, democracy, the League of Nations? Sure they exist—what of it? It still seemed to us that we were outside of history. We watched it all as if it were taking place on a stage; the play entertained us, made us laugh, at times even moved us, but not for one moment did it incorporate itself permanently into our lives.

Nevertheless—and I was already aware of this by then, though probably not very distinctly—there was another reason why the ablest and most intelligent of my companions preferred to remain on the sidelines, using jokes, mockery, and shrugs of the shoulder to keep from getting involved in anything—and if they did take something on, it seemed to be reluctantly and only for a laugh. This peculiar sort of bashfulness was the fault of the accursed secondary nature of our culture in relation to other, dominant cultures. At that time (as today too, unfortunately) our main goal was to *match* them, because when we achieved independent statehood it turned out that we were backward, behind the times, and we had to catch up with the nations in the first rank. The English or the French are unfamiliar with such problems; they come into direct contact with life and reality. We on the other hand were marching in the second rank; before us was not raw life but only the backs of those stepping out ahead of us. This freshly minted Poland, then, had to leave to others great discoveries in philosophy, science, and art, technological and other breakthroughs; we were consigned to the role of the pupil whose greatest achievement can be at best the rapid assimilation of others' accomplishments. Today in Poland, in this respect things are no better and in fact a lot worse. We've never been so lacking in self-dependency. But forty years ago too this hopeless secondariness barred our access to life and to reality.

*

Before long the four stories I'd written were joined by others. I hid these treasures in a locked drawer, since I was extremely shy when it came to my literary beginnings. But these new stories were ever bolder in terms of technique; I was enthusiastically moving toward a kind of writing that was not merely fantastic but was removed from reality. Removed? How should that be understood? Let me explain in a few words my process, which incidentally was not and is not mine exclusively, though a quarter of a century ago it constituted something new that many a reader was unable to stomach.

A writer can, if he wishes, describe reality as he sees it or as he imagines it to be; this produces realistic works such as the books of Sienkiewicz. But he can also apply a different method in which reality is reduced to its component parts, after which these parts are used like bricks to construct a new edifice, a new world or microcosm, which ought to be different from the regular world and yet correspond with it in some way . . . different but, as the physicists say, adequate.

Thus, for example, in my story "Dinner at Countess Pavahoke's" I invented a group of aristocrats sharing a series of exclusively vegetarian dinners in order to cultivate various kinds of sublimity and mental refinement; yet the swine of a cook serves them soup made from a little boy—and they consume it with relish. Nonsense, is it not? But it's nonsense composed of elements taken from life; it's a caricature of reality. How delightful it was to see this nonsense blossom beneath my pen, grow with its own inexorable logic, and lead to unforeseen resolutions.

I should mention in passing that this story, "Dinner at Countess Pavahoke's"—or "Countess Kotłubaj's" in Polish—almost got me involved in an affair of honor; for the Kotłubaj family, whose roots were somewhere in Lithuania, decided to call me out because of the various games I had played with their name in my story. The true source of my inspiration, however, was not them but a philanthropist and esthete well-known in Warsaw back then, the heiress Marta Krasińska.

Soon I had enough material for a book of stories. There were seven of them in all. Some of them turned out decidedly differently from what was being written in Poland at the time, but I was a long way from regarding myself as an innovator. In the circle of my friends—Breza, Adaś and Zosia Mauersberger, Tonio Sobański, to name those whose opinion I sought—the stories were enthusiastically received, and this encouraged me to publish them, though at the same time I wasn't at all eager to do so—I saw this as an extremely disagreeable step that I was obliged to take since it constituted an unavoidable consequence of writing. One day I went to see Kister, a well-known publisher and owner of the Rój press, and showed him my manuscript.

He required that I cover half the printing costs. I agreed, for what else could I do?

There remained the question of the title. I insisted on calling the book *Recollections of Adolescence;* I thought such a title would make people curious and at the same time indicate that I myself did not regard these stories as a definitive achievement.

Today I would not bet three cents that the direction of my entire future career as a writer was not determined at that moment. *Habent sua fata* titles too. Because my modesty and lack of confidence came back to haunt me. It turned out that these innocent stories considerably exceeded the intellectual and artistic capacity of the overwhelming majority of Polish critics of the time. They understood little or nothing in the stories themselves but found in the awkward title a capital excuse. It was said: the stories of a young author, who is still not entirely mature, as he himself acknowledges by calling his book *Recollections of Adolescence.* Let us hope that the author will improve and that his subsequent works will be more polished and mature. I was tormented by this immaturity to such an extent that it became the point of departure for my next book, *Ferdydurke,* and in this way I was gradually transformed into a specialist in this matter, and into its high priest.

Recollections of Adolescence appeared in 1933. Who else debuted at the same time as me? Michał Choromański had appeared in literature amid a great hoopla a little earlier—a year or two before, I believe. Along with me, Adolf Rudnicki began his literary career with a book entitled *The Rats,* and also Pola Gojawiczyńska; then, in the years immediately following, Jerzy Andrzejewski, Stefan Otwinowski, and the greatest star, Bruno Schulz. I shall have things to say about these writers, but first I'll recount the pains and joys of my own debut.

I felt uncomfortable as I gave a copy of my book, fresh from the oven, to my worthy family.

My mother thanked me politely, with alacrity even, yet not without embarrassment. My brothers received the gift with a restraint that did not bode well. There followed a few days of silence in the course of which they familiarized themselves with the contents of the work; but alas, this period could not be extended indefinitely, and the moment came when each of them said with the most natural expression they could muster: "You know, I just finished your book. It's a little too modern perhaps, but it's interesting. . . . I liked it . . . we'll have to see what the critics say. In any case, congratulations!"

I suspect that my relatives could not have been more embarrassed if I'd joined the ballet and begun to leap about the stage seminaked in front of an audience. They were a so-called decent family, and it was not clear what terrible sins they had committed to encounter such a disgrace. Being an artist is not a serious occupation—it's no kind of profession and no kind of social position; besides, a work of art almost always is of an intimate nature; it is in fact a kind of confession, which makes it difficult to swallow for the relatives and friends of the author. In addition to which, a beginning artist is always a rather pretentious phenomenon; it's as if a person had declared himself to be a candidate for greatness. It should come as no surprise, then, that neither I nor they felt particularly at ease.

If they had at least been able to some extent to appreciate my work! But these were not ordinary stories, written according to a formula, but something that broke away from the norm. If the truth be told, I myself, the author, was not really aware of what I'd written—so how could they be! It seems to me that they acted very wisely under the circumstances, relying on a calculation of probability. The chances that *Recollections* was a masterpiece were minimal, whereas it was most likely that after playing at literature for a shorter or longer time I'd return to more serious pursuits such as the law. As for me, I understood them perfectly and was no less embarrassed at the sight of that accursed book, which had put me at the mercy of every reader. But I knew I had to struggle through this. I'd lived too long in artificial isolation, and it was time to show who I was!

Thus began my first literary encounter with the world. In the papers there slowly began to appear notes and reviews. Some of them were highly enthusiastic, for example Breza's article in *Kurier Poranny,* but there was also no lack of fearfully negative or, even worse, dismissive ones. I was shot down by Kaden-Bandrowski, who described my writing as young, immature, pretentious, mannered, whereas Nowaczyński cheered me up by saying that each of the stories was a little masterpiece. Then what, in the end? Masterpieces or rubbish? It was enough to drive one insane! Depending on which newspaper you read, I was treated with pity or congratulated and commended.

How agonizing this whole gauntlet was for an ambitious young person! I was convulsed with anger as I came under fire from these unceremonious judgments, and it wouldn't have been strange if I had utterly lost confidence in myself. But if an artist has an inner conviction, even if only half-consciously, that what he's doing is good and important, it's enough that one or two people offer confirmation for him to be certain that his work is capable of being read the way he intended.

*

November 28, 1960

Publishing my first book, all the reviews and notices in the press— none of this yet meant a lasting entry into the literary circles of Warsaw. Slowly however, people began to emerge who were linked to me by a shared debut and a shared literary destiny. First to report was Adolf Rudnicki.

The phone rings. "Is that Mr. Witold Gombrowicz? My name is Rudnicki. Adolf. You know, I wrote a book: *The Rats*. We have the same occupation, what? Perhaps we could talk."

Today Adolf is one of Poland's leading writers, so it won't be amiss to recount how he seemed to me then, in 1933 I think it was, when I first met him. Slim, swarthy, animated, with a not too obviously Semitic appearance, effusive, sincere . . . I observed immediately that Adolf, to use a provocative expression, was not especially distinguished; there was no question but that he was from the suburbs, and not particularly respectable ones at that—in light of which I did my best to crush him with my supposedly aristocratic manner. If someone were to ask why I played the fool in such a way, my response would be that it was not foolishness but precisely intelligence that led me astray. As is common knowledge, an intelligent person is contrary, and, in accordance with the dialectical nature of his mind, always seeks the other side of the coin. In those days democracy, equality, progress, antigentry sentiment, and similar watchwords were already the currency of the age, especially in intellectual spheres; hence the temptation to appear before Adolf in a deliberately anachronistic guise.

Fortunately his intelligence and sense of humor were sufficient for him to perceive the game I was playing and not be too upset by it. We studied each other curiously. If, as Schopenhauer believed, it is touching to see the curiosity with which young people of the opposite sex gaze at one another in search of the future mother or father of their children, then the critical gaze with which two young artists measure each other when they first meet is also not without a deeper and more intimate significance. Each of them sees the other as a rival and seeks to test his own strengths on him, to discover whether his mental worth and his form are strong enough to endure. And so Adolf and I, still untried and inexperienced, but already filled with powerful ambitions, stared at each other surreptitiously, searching in our adversary for confirmation of our own superiority.

He had the upper hand because he knew my book, whereas I had not yet seen a copy of *The Rats*. I remember rather clearly certain impressions from that first conversation. I noticed—not without a sense of disappointment—that this meeting of two exceptional intellects was not devoid of a certain pettiness of a prosaic, middle-class character. To put it simply, Adolf was compensating with his mien. With his directness, his effusiveness, his sincerity he was covering up evident shortcomings in his upbringing and education, attempting to raise himself to the level of the higher social spheres. And he emphasized his own "talent" to conceal his cultural deficiencies. At that time I wasn't yet familiar with types such as Adolf, as Uniłowski, outstanding in some respects, and in others utterly unskilled. I still bore within me the tradition of the preceding generation of gentleman-writers like Sienkiewicz, Prus, Wyspiański, or even Przybyszewski, who were well brought up and refined; so it was with consternation and a certain suspicion that I stared at Adolf's feet in their worn shoes stretched out in front of him, I would say, terrifyingly, while their owner talked his head off, not always with great eloquence.

I suspect that he too must have been alarmed by the specimen he saw before him—those games of mine, calculated for effect, my conscious artificiality, all those complications with which I masked myself. But what do you expect? A person beginning to write books is a person, as the expression goes, in a delicate situation, especially one starting off, as we were, in a country whose culture did not yet have a defined look or style. It was this ambiguous situation that made playacting necessary, though it would obviously have been better to avoid it.

I immediately took a dislike to Adolf's sentimentalism—not only because it was a masquerade, but because the mascarade was in poor taste. He was too expansive, too "melodious" one might say, awash in a vague sort of lyricism; he lacked an awareness of the absurdity of certain things. Once he showed me a letter from a female admirer who called him Dolf. I burst into sarcastic laughter: This "Dolf" seemed awfully comical and provincial to me. "You're terrible," exclaimed Adolf, hurriedly putting the letter away, and already in love.

Despite this, we quickly became close, since we had many worries in common: the critics, *Wiadomości Literackie,* supporters and enemies—there was so much to talk about. But I knew he hadn't really liked my book. He appreciated it—for its modernness, its structure—but for him it still was not "it," it was "weak," "too sleek." He once said to me, "You're so thin . . . so thin you can only be seen in profile." His opinion in this regard expressed the misunderstanding that was slowly arising between me and the majority of the Polish intelligentsia.

Power was what was demanded. Whatever in literature was delicate, subtle, psychologically or artistically refined, and understated, met with scorn or even pity. This was not what Poland needed! The drive for power, even violence, was at bottom proof of weakness: It meant quite simply that Poles, still highly unsure of themselves and their continued existence, sought in books what they lacked in life— power. It's just that in literature, in art, things are sometimes the opposite to real life. Any weakling can roar like a lion on paper, where mighty phrases cost little; whereas a delicacy like that of Chopin's, for example—dogged in the extreme, intense, calculated—demands uncommon effort and an uncommon character. A poem by Verlaine, that almost melts in the mouth, is in this sense more powerful than the bombastic prose of our Kaden-Bandrowski.

Adolf too longed for such a literature—strong, immediate, lashing, wounding—though of course his taste in this respect was much more refined. When I set about reading *The Rats,* I noticed in addition something that made me a little skeptical. It was an odd book, delirious, a rant from beginning to end, a sort of inner monologue that was predatory, profound, vertiginous. The writer's talent was plain to see; this prose had vigor and it had claws. It was just that it was too "brilliant," it was too obvious that the author was nudging the reader in the ribs and winking: You see, I'm a great writer, maybe even a genius; this couldn't have been written by just anyone. It was a work that had no regard for anything, above all for the reader, and it impressed one precisely with this scorn.

I confess that it bored me at once; I stopped reading after three or four pages. It wouldn't surprise me if Adolf had read my *Recollections* in the same way. Then came the inevitable conversation.

"What did you think of it?"

"Well, of course you have talent . . . but things haven't fallen into place yet."

The conversations we had as young writers always ran like this. There was a mutual acknowledgment of talent, "and considerable talent at that," after which there followed a "but," shifting our greatness into the future and somewhat placing it under a question mark. It's interesting, though, that my little volume also contained the same desire for greatness, though it was no doubt realized differently than in Adolf's case. But this was typical of my generation. We were sick of the second-rate, or inferior, nature of Polish literature, and we yearned for something on a larger scale.

*

In that year of 1933, the year in which my first book was published, my father died. He had been ill for many months, but his condition worsened suddenly, and when he passed away only my mother and I were present. It wasn't till the following day that my brothers arrived from the country.

This death left me with a rather shameful memory. When he died, I tried to embrace my mother so as in this way at least to show my feelings; but the gesture came out awkwardly, and in the blink of an eye the entire abjectness of my situation was revealed to me: I was incapable of ordinary human reactions, of sincerity, tenderness; I was as it were paralyzed by form, style, by this whole accursed manner that I'd created for myself . . . and here I was, incapable of offering my own mother a little warmth at such a moment! Relations were distant in our family; we were too critical, ironic, sarcastic; our sense of the ridiculous was too great, and this killed any more intense response in us. I'm speaking of myself and my brothers, since both the women—my sister and my mother—were rather victims of this state of affairs. But my father had an uncommunicative, Lithuanian nature, and his relations with us were not close.

When my brothers appeared and there began the complicated process of arranging the funeral, a macabre mixture of grief and social, even financial, affairs, along with common snobbery (how should the obituary look in the *Kurier Warszawski*? who would speak at the service?), my distaste and anger took precedence over all my other feelings. I didn't reproach myself or my brothers that we were not able to grasp the fact of the death right away. After all, no one is in control of their feelings, and besides, sentiment had to find its own, more intimate moment. But I was irked by our powerlessness in the face of form and its conventional demands, and by the docility with which we donned funereal expressions, even though in our black suits we really were grief-stricken.

Yes, at the funeral I was racked by dismal reflections. Our family was coming to an end. Appearances to the contrary, and despite the fact that my brothers had married and had children, it was a family in decline; the unhealthy blood of the Kotkowskis, which we had inherited from our mother and which burdened us with the possibility of psychological disturbances, was probably the direct cause of the disorder. My father was the last of the Gombrowiczes who enjoyed respect and inspired confidence; we, the next generation, were eccentrics of whom it was said, "What a pity they didn't take after old Gombrowicz." Concerning myself I had no illusions: I knew I was a kind of psychological cripple for whom a normal existence was out of the question, and who had to seek his own path. Sensitivity, imagination, complexes, fears, and obsessions preyed on me all the more as they were concealed from view, and perhaps that's why I felt so bad about looking well and even contented. But truth be told, there was no straightforward path for me, and I knew that if I didn't justify myself in my own eyes and those of others with some higher accomplishment, nothing remained for me but to descend to the level of a garden-variety degenerate.

These were sharp, harsh, hurtful thoughts, which visited me at other times too; and I regard them as having great significance in my entire development. In Poland, by and large, no one was aware of the connections between art (and the whole life of the mind in general) and sickness. On this subject an astounding optimism reigned amongst us; for Poles, an artist was not "a neurotic carrying out his own course of treatment," as Freud had it, but a fellow who creates out of an excess of well-being and vital forces, with the help of a special gift of the gods called talent. According to this account, art arises not from illness but from health. This superficial optimism has spread to the artists themselves—how often have I met poets, painters, or writers who were real clinical cases, up to their ears in pathologies, yet utterly convinced that there was nothing wrong with them and even that they could be models for others. The fact that I never deluded myself and always remained fully aware of my infirmities allowed me to situate my writing in a more real and tragic climate; but it also allowed me to obtain a distance on my sickness, and who knows if this didn't give me a clearer feeling of healthiness and normality. For a sick man knows more about health than a healthy man, just as a hungry man knows more about bread.

After my father's death the eight-room apartment on Służewska Street was too big for my mother and sister. They moved to a smaller, very pleasant apartment on Chocimska, with a view of Wilanów; I took a place close by, in the same building. In this way I was able to take my meals at my mother's, which had its advantages.

At the time I was working on opus number two, the comedy *Princess Ivona*. I don't know if it will be of interest to my future biographers that I wrote a good portion of *Ivona* lying on the rug in the living room on Służewska Street. This strange position came about because I had to keep an eye on my father, who was in bed in the next room, already only semiconscious, and prone to considerable nervous agitation.

I wrote *Ivona* with great difficulty and great reluctance. I decided to exploit for the theater the technique I'd developed in my stories— the capacity for devising a disconnected and often absurd motif, a little like a musical motif. What was coming out for me was a scathing absurdity that was quite unlike the plays being written at the time. I struggled unrelentingly with form. Those awful hours spent immobile in front of a sheet of paper, when the pen is idle and the imagination desperately seeks solutions, while the whole emerging edifice creaks and threatens to collapse!

At that time I also began to be drawn into journalism. The initiative came from the magazine *Polska Zbrojna*, whose editor had published an exceedingly enthusiastic review of *Recollections of Adolescence;* he subsequently asked me to write a column for him. At this point I came to realize that being a columnist was an entirely different kettle of fish! All my artistic skills were insufficient for those damned articles, which were a dead loss. The editor had soon had enough. Sometime later Miedziński, the editor of *Gazeta Polska,* who along with other personages from government circles used to take part in my brothers' hunting parties, offered me some work; this time something suddenly clicked in me. I developed a flair for newspaper writing, I tossed off a few articles like no one's business, and people began to congratulate me. What of it, though, since my next article was rejected. I discontinued the supply. I was financially independent. This was a great and perhaps somewhat immoral phrase. I could thumb my nose at everything!

At last *Ivona* was finished. I asked Adaś Mauersberger's advice on what to do with it.

"Show it to Mira," he said. "She's the most intelligent actress I know, and she has a fine understanding of the theater. She'll tell you if it can be played, and who you should give it to."

Mira Zimińska was indeed intelligent, and witty too. However, I had my reasons for concern, since with actors, and especially actresses, I was in a state of war. Was it because, as I was fond of saying in theater circles, someone who puts on faces in public is not a respectable person? No, the real reason was deeper and more hidden. I didn't like performers: I considered them a lower category of artist, and it angered me that they enjoyed greater fame and recognition than true creators. This was probably one more manifestation of my inner protest against second-rateness in art, which irritated me all the more because it made me think of our Polish second-rateness in world culture. But I was even more critical of actresses than of actors and was in the habit of pretending that I didn't know them—I would introduce myself to each one every time I met them. Once, when for the fifth time I presented myself courteously and with a gallant bow to a certain diva, she immediately seized a glass of water and poured it over my head.

Mira luckily was not set against me. But her theatrical horizons were insufficiently broad for her to appreciate an innovative play like *Ivona*. She told me that the beginning wasn't bad, but that the rest was hopeless.

*

February 2, 1961

On New Year's Eve, to bid farewell to 1934 I organized an artistic booze-up in my mother's apartment on Chocimska. My mother and sister were in the country at the time, and so I could do what I wished in the apartment. The party, which lasted till six in the morning, was a visible indication of my sound position in the literary circles of Warsaw. I no longer remember exactly who the guests were, but they certainly included Breza, the Mauersbergers, and Tonio Sobański; Rudnicki was there, and I think Choromański too; there was the brotherhood of topers led by Światek Karpiński and "Minio," in other words, Janusz Minkiewicz; there was a sprinkling of actresses, Zdzisław Czermański, Kanarek (who today is a well-known painter in the United States); and maybe Witkacy and perhaps Bruno Schulz. I was under the influence, like everyone there, and pretended to be having a good time; but this didn't stop me from realizing once again how far my nature was from this kind of merriment.

I didn't know how to enjoy myself in this way. I had "bad alcohol," as was explained to me by the great expert Światek Karpiński—mine was a hypochondriac and hepatic alcohol that didn't connect me to anyone, but on the contrary, alienated me. This melancholy property was not, of course, without influence on my literary destiny, since in Poland it's easier to imagine a writer without a pen than one without a glass in his hand. That doesn't mean that I did not keep company with drinkers and didn't have companions and even friends amongst them; yet it was always a qualified friendship, a little forced and often somewhat false. I never knew how to get excited about the antics of those friends of mine: When it was recounted how Światek, in a drunken haze, took some fish up and down in an elevator "to give them a good time," or how Minio was left penniless after a night of libations and so at seven in the morning stood outside Miss Plater's highly respectable school for young ladies and, with hat in hand, begged the arriving schoolgirls for a couple of pennies so he could at least buy some vodka—I appreciated the humor of these situations, but as it were from a distance.

This brotherhood in intoxication—Światek, Minio, Dołęga-Mostowicz, Jurkowski, and many others—was perhaps one of the most distinctive features of the Warsaw of that time. Today I would call them "precursors," since those wise men seemed to have read clearly in the book of fate, and so they drowned in vodka the absurdity of the Polish situation, the tragic inevitability that cast doubt on any honest effort. To the best of my knowledge, today that lushes' league has many members in Poland, and they have their own good reasons for being there. In those days, the band of poet-drinkers was brought together under the banner of mockery, jokes, word play, fun and games, and witty stories; they took nothing seriously except vodka and women. Not even finances! Though they also had a talent for money-making and could wring a buck from anything. Światek Karpiński, a poet—the only real poet amongst them—provided texts for the cabarets; he collaborated with Minkiewicz on an annual Christmas pantomime, and he wrote comic rhyming epigrams for *Kurier Warszawski*. All this secured him a sizable income, which he liquidated in various nighttime establishments. He used to claim that jokes were entirely a matter of technique and that he had a method of manufacturing them in any amount, on demand. As for Janusz Minkiewicz, he was a poet too, but of a lighter caliber, a poet-songwriter in the Parisian style, with what is called charm. He affected an indolent, languid, slow, catlike air, virtually purring those jokes of his. He was Światek's best friend, and a significant part of what he earned was thanks to Światek. The third of these musketeers, Dołęga-Mostowicz, had a considerable income from his trashy novels, dashed off "for a broader public" and devoid of any artistic pretensions. He lived handsomely in a side wing of the Poznańskis' palace on the Aleje Ujazdowskie; he had a soft spot for antiques, and he gave weekly "five o'clock teas," which began on Tuesdays at five in the afternoon and ended on Thursday morning with the entire company, including the host, lying paralytic on the sumptuous marble floor. Who did not take part in those events! There I would meet the Halam gang, famous from the ballet, Wiech, the Prince of Hohenlohe, and goodness knows who else!

Jurkowski manufactured cheap romance novels, like Dołęga-Mostowicz, and was a kind of back-up Dołęga, in my eyes at least.

As I mentioned, the object of worship of the assemblage was "a sense of humor." Whoever lacked it had no business there. It was through humor that the endless consumption of alcohol approached salvation. Since my first book had earned the full approval of the booze-befuddled jokesters, I was someone they appreciated, and even—after *Ferdydurke*—admired. And so I was plied with vodka, with great feeling, almost with maternal warmth, as if in the expectation that at any moment I would come out with some magnificent "line"—which never happened, since lines were not my specialty.

For an author like me, not popular, and more accustomed to receiving brickbats than praise, such warm acknowledgment was very moving; but I always took care not to allow myself to be bought over, and it even afforded me a sinister pleasure when someone who respected and loved me was rewarded with my merciless criticism. To be frank, Minio's charms, Światek's poeticality, or Dołęga-Mostowicz's drunken flights of imagination engendered repulsion more than feelings of friendship in me. What was it that so repelled me? The sybaritism? The lasciviousness? The softness, the flaccidity, the crumpledness of that fraternity? The stupidity of the females, who were often good-looking, and who allowed themselves to be taken in by the trappings of art and intellect? The cheapness of the poetry, calculatedly written to obtain whores and money? The often triumphal self-satisfaction of those smooth operators who knew how to milk the bourgeoisie?

In sexual matters I'm no Cato; I would say that in such things, for me more important than the sin itself is "how" one sins, and above all "who" is sinning. I'm prepared to forgive a great deal in fresh and bewitching individuals; whereas the excesses of bloated, inebriated men do not enthuse me, and I was disgusted to see girls worthy of a better fate falling for the lures of such fellows. Above all, I held it against those poets that they had virtually no poetry in them, and that the little they had, they did not respect.

They may have had other good qualities of which I was unaware, and which incidentally could not have manifested themselves in that lifestyle of theirs, which took place between the Adria and the Zodiak. In a social sense too they constituted a rather disgraceful phenomenon. It's well known that the measure of a nation's culture is not its highest art, which is the creation of exceptional individuals, but precisely its second-rank literature, in which good manners, both on the part of the author and of the reader, can be more important than talent. None of this set was an artist on a larger scale and none of them could harbor any pretentions to excellence, but despite this their writing could have carried the marks of decency that distinguish an educated, well-read person with some discernment and a disciplined imagination from an ordinary producer of trash. Unfortunately, the popular novels of Dołęga-Mostowicz and Jurkowski, with the possible exception of *The Career of Nikodem Dyzma,* were written for the gutter, the Warsaw gutter, and for the factory workers. Karpiński's epigrams and articles, and Minkiewicz's epigrams and songs, had the appearance of solid workmanship—those two cultivated their métier and like a respectable business they didn't sell shoddy merchandise. And yet this too was an unkempt, disordered world, anarchic in the Russian way—they weren't bad people, but they lacked that reflex of a cultured person which is a matter of heredity, upbringing, and tradition, and often successfully substitutes for a lack of an outlook on life, of morality and faith. From year to year they wallowed deeper in licentiousness and all the mean tricks that go with it; from year to year they were more broken, drunker, and more desperate. Right until the war came along.

*

Every evening around nine I'd head out to the café—the Ziemiańska, which was popular in those days. I would sit at a table, order a "small black" coffee and wait till my café companions gathered.

A café can become an addiction just as vodka can. For a real habitué, not to go to the café at the designated time is simply to fall ill. In a short time I became such a fanatic that I set aside all my other evening activities, including the theater, movies, and my social life. It must be added that a Warsaw café, and the Ziemiańska in particular, was not like other cafés of the world. One entered from the street into darkness, a fearful haze of smoke and stale air, from which abyss there loomed astonishing faces striving to communicate by shouts and gestures in the ever-present din. The aquiline features of various *schöngeists,* in other words intellectual aesthetes, fraternized with honest, round, peasant mugs from the country that had arrived the day before from Lublin or Lwów province; there were also wily faces of shysters from the suburbs, and occasionally one glimpsed the walrus mustache of a country squire—for this was a café of poets, and poets are born everywhere, like vermin.

The Ziemiańska had its own hierarchy. In the intellectual sense it was a multistoreyed edifice, and it wasn't so easy to transplant oneself from a lower floor to a higher one.

The first floor was composed of a variety of young people, beginners who were not yet known and generally had no right to speak; and also other supporters, mostly recruited from the semi-intelligentsia, whose lack of education and polish made it difficult for them to take part in the symposia. They were somewhat like a Greek chorus, but a voiceless one that was important simply by its presence—when a handful of speechless enthusiasts silently joined a particular group, this meant that at the table in question noteworthy things would happen, for these were connoisseurs who didn't miss a single paper share at this literary stock market. When it transpired that my table's stocks were rising, such folk immediately began to pull their chairs up with the air of people taking a seat in the front rows of the theater. Night after night this took place in absolute silence; only once in a while would someone cough or giggle.

The second floor was above all the "poets of the proletariat." This name included not just working-class bards but also those who, originating in the lower social spheres, had become worshippers of all sorts of surrealism, Dadaism, and other such ultramodernism, with which they compensated for the more glaring problems arising from their primitivism and backwardness. They took part in discussions, but not without difficulty, since they usually had only one hobbyhorse to ride—for instance, Marxism, or the esthetics of Peiper's poetry, or psychoanalysis—and all the other horses of humanity were unknown to them. It must be admitted that the overwhelming majority of the Ziemiańska's regulars fell into this rather uncomfortable category. The ignorance of these intellectuals was quite incredible; from a mixture of concepts and readings, from scraps and pieces acquired here and there in no order, there sprang up fantastical understandings, like Falstaff's cloud taking on ever different shapes.

The next floor up comprised those who already had a "name": authors and artists whose stocks had been noted, though they couldn't yet claim to be famous. And at the very top—even literally, for they occupied the mezzanine, elevated above the crowd—was the glorious table of the Skamandrists: Słonimski, Tuwim, Iwaszkiewicz, Wieniawa-Długoszowski, and other great figures, bandying their jokes about.

My manner in the Ziemiańska was characterized by a nonchalance clearly signaling that I'd no need to "earn a living by the pen" and thus to hurry my writing career along too anxiously. I hardly ever joined the Skamandrists, since I wasn't yet on an even footing with them, and I could not allow myself to behave with them the way I would have liked. In fact, I was not fussy about my choice of company; who joined my table was really a matter of some indifference to me, and I was quite happy even with the more grotesque semi-intellectuals, since they constituted a much more unpredictable and poetic element than folk in straight neckties and well-trimmed noggins. With a blush of modesty, but also with justifiable pride, I can say that I soon acquired considerable popularity in the Ziemiańska, and my table was frequently visited by a sizable crowd of fans, who took their places at it even before I arrived. My jokes, facial expressions, sayings, my dialectics, my poetic flights of fancy, my philosophical and psychological reasoning, artistic declarations, crushing attacks, and insidious provocations—all this electrified my listeners, and mostly because it happened to be the antithesis of the accepted norm in the Ziemiańska. I was not a great lover of poetry; I was neither excessively progressive, nor modern; I was not a typical intellectual, nor a nationalist, nor a Catholic, nor a communist, not a right-winger; I didn't worship science, or art, or Marx. Then what was I at that time? Most often, I was the negation of my disconcerted interlocutor, who only after many sittings realized that I was discussing for sport, for amusement, and also out of curiosity, just to investigate the reverse of every thesis. That contrariness, which had remained from discussions with my mother in my youth, gave my dialogues a high-spirited imaginativeness, and at the same time sometimes led us into truly unexpected territory. I suspect that the amount of nonsense, claptrap, and hogwash uttered by me in the Ziemiańska reached astronomical proportions; and yet through all this insanity there shone my natural common sense and the clear-headedness, the realism that was so alert in me. For all my eccentricities, my behavior in the Ziemiańska had entirely solid foundations and, I believe, was in fact far from being foolish.

I needed victims. I was happy to chance upon some naive and fervent individual with whom I could toy like a cat playing with a mouse. And it sometimes happened that these victims became admirers, even friends—it was in this way I acquired the circle that in later years included Stefan Otwinowski and his wife, Ewa; the poet Staś Piętak; Lipiński, the editor of *Szpilki*, and his wife; Jerzy Pietrkiewicz; and others. At times there were brief conflicts when things got out of hand and one or another person would jump up with a clatter and leave in a huff. But generally speaking, people were more often entertained than offended.

I shall return again to my activities in the Ziemiańska, the Ipsa, and the Zodiak, since in time they acquired substance; I even dare think that they weren't wholly without influence on the literary atmosphere of the country. This claim may seem exaggerated to many serious literati from those times, but it must be explained that I operated almost exclusively on the lower floor—the upper one knew virtually nothing about what was going on there. Once Boy-Żeleński, a seasoned frequenter of cafés, grabbed me by the sleeve: "I hear, sir, that you rule over the Ziemiańska, and that you won't allow any of us in!" It was true: I held the fort, I was prophet, maestro, and clown, but only amongst individuals like me who had not fully "arrived" and who were unpolished and inferior. I preferred not to associate with the others, the worthies, with whom I could never allow myself to joke, make fun, or provoke, on whom I couldn't impose my own style; they bored me and I knew that I bored them. Yet many of those who had not yet arrived finally did so, and even occupied leading positions. Today, reading certain Polish books I sometimes come across passages that might not have been written without those conversations back then. What's soaked up by the youthful shell, in later age becomes its smell.

Associating with me was always, as it is today, rather difficult, because as a rule I aim at debate and conflict; I try to lead the discussion in such a way as to make it risky, sometimes even unpleasant and embarrassing and indiscreet, because such an approach engages both my personality and that of my interlocutor. The pleasant, calm, gentle conversation usually found in literary circles always seemed to me to be mortally insipid and unworthy of those who are intellectually alert.

*

February 6, 1961

Here's a strange thing: I cannot recall how I first met Bruno Schulz. Was it at one of Zofia Nałkowska's gatherings? No, I believe he telephoned me to say he had read my *Recollections of Adolescence* and would like to talk with me.

But I can see him as he was when I first laid eyes on him: a tiny little fellow. Small and timid, with an oh-so-quiet voice; inconspicuous, mild, yet with something cruel and severe concealed behind an almost childlike gaze.

This little fellow was the most outstanding artist of all those I knew in Warsaw. He was immeasurably greater than Kaden, Nałkowska, Goetel, and so many other literary academicians who glittered with honors and dominated the press and the salons of the capital. The prose that came from his pen was imaginative and immaculate; amongst us he was the most European writer, with the right to take his place amongst the greatest intellectual and artistic aristocracy of Europe. And yet, when I met him—and it was [after] the publication of his book *Cinnamon Shops*—Bruno was a modest schoolteacher in Drohobycz who had come to the capital for a couple of months, a vulnerable creature for whom people felt sorry. He remained such a browbeaten provincial teacher till his tragic death in a German camp. And I'm afraid that today, for reasons I shall explain in a moment, it's too late for his art to be appreciated in the West. And in

Poland, who knows him today? A few hundred poets? A handful of writers? He has remained what he was, a prince traveling incognito.

At that time, when he came to my apartment on Służewska Street, his literary position was nevertheless much more solid than mine. He hadn't reached a broader readership, but the elite knew him and held him in high regard. Yet Bruno's masochistic nature drove him to remove himself to the background. He preferred admiring to being admired. Quietly, confidentially, with a goodness that was nevertheless strange—I might say that it was at bottom hard—he began by singing my praises.

"What a book! I'm bowled over by your short stories. I'd never be capable of writing anything like this myself."

Later on I found out, not without chagrin, that Bruno was generous with his enthusiasm for other writers too—and not only because he liked to bring people pleasure. In that provincial fellow there dwelled a desire for luxury, for lofty hierarchies, for glory and pride. And yet the almost painful severity one sensed perhaps not even so much in him as in his vicinity, as if lurking in the corner, compelled me to take his opinions concerning my writing most seriously. And I was soon to learn that these were not empty phrases—no one showed me so much magnanimous friendship or stood by me so fervently.

This was the beginning of numerous conversations, hardly ever on personal topics. Bruno brought from Drohobycz an insatiable thirst for mental and intellectual companionship; in this he was sometimes feverish and wearisome. He asked and listened—I opened up and expatiated—he commented, clarified, and got to the heart of the matter, posing even newer questions. From the first moment he assumed a rather passive attitude in respect to me, of one who gathers information and asks questions. It might have seemed that he was destined to play second fiddle. Yet his capacity for focus and his intensity, a sort of extraordinary acceptance of his own fate, his own destiny, the demonic power of his passion, which arose somewhere in the sexual sphere and for this reason was so tragic and ardent, made his modest head-nodding into something more momentous. And it was enough to open his book to find an entirely different Schulz: majestic, with sentences that were weighty and magnificent, unraveling gradually like the dazzling tail of the peacock, a poet with inexhaustible powers of creating metaphors, exceptionally sensitive to form, and capable of modulations and gradations, rendering his ironically Baroque prose like a song. Many of the artistic tasks he set himself were utterly perilous; yet he never came to grief. Nevertheless, in my continued contacts with him I discovered two flaws that weakened his range. First, he was too much a poet and only a poet; because of this his prose, laden with metaphor, partially gave the impression of a mistake that should have been categorized as poetry, his true element. And second, like all Polish poets he was utterly helpless beyond metaphor; he couldn't deal with the real world and was incapable of assimilating it. He had developed his own form, which was narrow if infinitely deep, and he was unable to write differently or to go beyond his own rather meager subject matter.

Such people achieve great things when they are original. But Bruno followed in the footsteps of Kafka, with whom he shared his Semitic blood, and though in many ways he was innovative, it's hard to deny that the other man's vision impregnated his world too. This is why I do not predict a worldwide success for his work, which today is translated into foreign languages, even though it's won the admiration of many eminent English and French readers.

From me he differed principally in the fact that, though like him I was concerned with form, I aimed to break it up and I sought to broaden my literature so it could encompass ever more phenomena, whereas he shut himself up in his form as in a fortress, or a prison.

I've never met anyone less envious, and more magnanimously generous. It must be confessed that envy is a common quality of writers; but they are intelligent, and to a great extent this civilizes their potential uncouthness. In most cases they will not do harm, but neither will they raise a finger to help a rival's ascent to Parnassus. Bruno's wonderful unselfishness appeared in all its glory when my third book, the novel *Ferdydurke*, came out. His first encounter with it was not a particularly happy one.

I gave him the manuscript, which was far from being finished, during one of his visits to Warsaw. A few days later he told me gently, though with his perpetually present severity or sharpness in the tortuous background, "I'd advise you to drop this. You should go back to the other genre, from the *Recollections of Adolescence*, which you mastered so brilliantly. I don't think this should be published."

A cold shiver ran down my spine.

No one besides him had read this novel, into which I'd put so much work. Bruno was the first. I trusted him. And it should not be forgotten that *Ferdydurke* was a venture into virgin territory, an attempt to discover new lands, to carve out new pathways—in a word, a risky endeavor that could not be fully under control. Damn it! Perhaps it really was without value? Two years of labor! So much hope!

I was close to throwing it in the trash. But I summoned up enough heroism to keep on pushing my barrow. A year or so later the book was ready and I sent one of the first copies to Bruno in Drohobycz. A miracle occurred. In the course of a single day I received several telegrams from him—because as he read, he kept running to the post office to send me new compliments. Then, when he came to Warsaw, a timid and soft-spoken Schulz delivered a lecture at the Writers Union in which, without especially raising his voice, he informed the gathered artists that a sun had arisen to extinguish all the stars. Well, well! The audience began to protest, and there was almost a scandal.

And yet we debuted together—and the genre of our writing made us rivals—and he was ten years older than I was! Such unselfishness is a rarity amongst writers.

One day he took me to visit Stanisław Ignacy Witkiewicz. And so it was that Witkiewicz, Schulz, and I—three people endeavoring to lead Polish literature in new directions—finally met in person.

I must contend with the fact that this memoir of mine from Poland is intended not only for those who are familiar with Polish literature but also for a broader audience; this makes it difficult to write about certain matters that were vital for me at the time, yet because of their complicated character are not always accessible to the uninitiated. Such an uninitiated person may never have heard of Stanisław Ignacy Witkiewicz, of Bruno Schulz, or of me either; for we made up a group of very difficult writers who were not especially popular and who stood in opposition to Polish literary life. Nevertheless it is time, two decades later, for the uninitiated to learn that this group of ours exerted a considerable influence on Polish art, and today has the greatest chance of all Polish prose of being known and appreciated in Europe and in the world. This is already history, in the past, and so I should be permitted to speak of it objectively and without false modesty.

Yet was this in fact a group? We were linked much more by public opinion than by connections amongst ourselves. Bruno and I were not close with Witkacy; and in essence, aside from the enthusiasm that the big-hearted Bruno lavished on me, skepticism and distance held sway amongst us. I didn't believe in Witkiewicz's art, whereas for him I was too much of a milksop, and he held no great expectations for me. As for Bruno, both Witkacy and I treated his writings with a certain reserve, and in Warsaw circles he had much more ardent admirers.

As I mentioned, Bruno took me to Witkacy's. We marched up to some floor off the courtyard of a building on Bracka Street. We rang the bell; I was somewhat on edge after hearing the stories going round about the eccentricities and extravagances of this man, who was gifted with such an outstanding mind. And here in the opened door there appeared an immense dwarf who began to grow before our eyes: It was Witkacy, who had opened the door from a squatting position and was slowly standing up. He liked practical jokes like this! I, on the other hand, did not find them amusing. From the very first moment Witkacy fatigued me and bored me. He was never at rest, always highly strung, tormenting himself and others with his perpetual playacting, his craving to shock and to draw attention to himself, forever cruelly and painfully playing with people. All these shortcomings, which I shared, I now observed as in a distorting mirror, turned monstrous and inflated to apocalyptic proportions.

He started to show us his "atrocity museum," the highlights of which included something he identified as the dried tongue of a newborn child, some hair that had allegedly belonged to Bejlis, and a letter from a nymphomaniac that was indeed revoltingly licentious.

I said, "Sir, please stop showing us these things! They're unseemly!"

He gazed at me intently.

"Unseemly?" he asked.

He was somewhat taken aback. And I had once again been overcome by my mania for being an artist and a Bohemian in the homes of the God-fearing gentry, but a member of the landed gentry and even of the nobility amongst Bohemians, intellectuals, and artists. Unseemly! It must have been years since this smoker of hashish and goodness knows what else, this morphine addict, megalomaniac, schizophrenic, paranoiac, jokester, cynic, pervert, Dadaist, and pseudo-madman had heard such naivety. Unseemly! For my part this was an instinct for self-defense; I knew that if I didn't stand up to Witkacy from the beginning he would devour me, dominate me, tie me to his chariot. He was incapable of being with people on an even footing. He had to be the luminary; if in company he ceased even for a second to be the center of attention, he would begin to languish. And so I was under no illusions and knew that if I didn't succeed in playing with this man, he would be the one playing with me. But what could I say to him that would truly take him by surprise? Then that sanctimonious word of the bourgeoisie and the gentry popped into my head: "unseemly."

And thus our roles were established: With Witkacy, I was always the representative of good manners and rural common sense. I confess, moreover, that I didn't do a good job of this at all. I was also pre-pared at any moment to sever relations with him; I knew that he often took offense and often offended others, and I decided not to tolerate this and to put an end instantly to our entire acquaintance if the need arose. It's truly bizarre that despite all this, our relations persisted for several years—perhaps because we communed better through our books than in person, and because we did in fact have a little respect for one another.

I rarely had the opportunity to observe Witkacy with Schulz, and I don't know much about their relations; but I imagine that Bruno, intense and as it were hardened, had even less to say to him than I did. That was actually the worst of it: Like a despotic ruler, that arch-egotist could not abide anyone who was someone; he surrounded himself with mediocrities, serfs, adulators, acolytes, even abom-inable scribblers, so long as they lay at his feet. I recall one season in Zakopane when Witkacy paraded around at the head of a veritable throng of such woebegone losers—it was a sight as embarrassing as it was irritating.

Nevertheless, let us try to define what it was that, despite all these contrasts and personal animosities, we had in common, and what constituted our worth. In my view, it was our desire to overcome Polish parochialism, to sail out onto the broadest waters. We lived for Europe and the world, in contrast to local stars such as Kaden-Bandrowski, Goetel, Boy-Żeleński, or Tuwim, who were a hundred times more Polish, better adapted to local readers, and hence more famous. We, for instance, knew the value of originality, and not on a local but a universal scale. We were looking for humanity as such, not local humanity, Polish humanity. We approached art as people versed in the boldest foreign techniques and concepts, ready for any-thing so long as we could seize the bull by the horns. We were more rigorous, colder, harsher, more dramatic, and also infinitely freer, because we had renounced many constraining loves.

This was our strength, yet also our weakness—for our shortcomings stood out all the more distinctly in light of the great tasks we set ourselves. It's perhaps not so difficult to become something of value within the nation; but to become someone in the world requires an uncommon effort. It often happens that a tiny fault renders the best machine ineffective, all the more when the machine is a precise one. Thus, Witkiewicz's intelligence was outstanding, his courage, persistence, relentlessness were magnificent; but I think he lacked a sense of immediate effect. Too often he was a theorist unaware that he bored people and annoyed them; he had no ability to interact with a living person rather than with abstraction, theory, form, and that drove him to stiffness, affectedness, even at times to cheap tricks. Schulz, on the other hand, was too confined by his perversions and his art, as if in an ivory tower; he probably had too much respect for art and was unable to enjoy it from a position of superiority. The form he had elaborated constrained him to such a degree that he was afraid to go a single step beyond it. My defects are not worth mentioning here; I'll have occasion more than once to return to them. Suffice it to say that all my inner work involved evading them— I wrote despite, *to* spite, my own indolence.

Witkacy the demon met a demonic end. Escaping from the Bolsheviks during the last war, he took poison in some forest. Nor was Schulz spared by his intimate, masochistic relations with suffering and pain: During the war, as a Jew he found himself in a concentration camp, but he was protected by a certain German who held a high-ranking position and was enchanted by Bruno's brilliant drawings. But another German fell out with Bruno's guardian and out of resentment [rest of text probably missing].

*

February 27, 1961

I was afraid in Poland. True, there was no particular threat; the borders of the state were fixed, foreign policy was tranquil, internal affairs were more or less in order, Piłsudski's government had a strong foundation for the long term; and yet it was like sitting on a powder keg. I'm speaking for myself. I think the only cause of this unease of mine was the fact that I felt we belonged to the East, that we were part of Eastern and not Western Europe. Yes; neither Catholicism, nor our idiosyncratic attitude to Russia, nor the links our culture had with Rome and Paris—none of this could do anything to combat the Asiatic destitution that was consuming us from below. Our entire culture was a flower pinned to a peasant's sheepskin coat. And what could the upper echelons do about it, even if they were to renounce utterly their egotism and were to be inspired by the most sublime intentions? Could our gentry, our industry, our intelligentsia make an impression on a peasant, or on a provincial town wallowing in mud? The financing of radical reforms was far beyond our capabilities. No one could do anything. Grousing about the people of that time, accusing them of failing to evince the necessary initiative, is in my view nonsensical. Poland was a young state taking its first steps. Europe was still in disorder; if one wished to avoid revolution, it was necessary to patch the holes any way one could, to play for time, and wait till the progress of organization and civilization in the world offered more favorable circumstances. As far as revolution was concerned, it was hard to delude oneself into thinking otherwise. It would have meant the ruin of everything that had been accomplished, the loss of independence, and the rule of brutal, uncontrollable forces that held no respect whatsoever for humankind. Yet there was hope that the country would pull itself up and become part of the Western system of prosperity.

But let me repeat what I said earlier: the Poland that was born out of the First World War was a land of paralyzed people. The most vital elements were condemned to provisionality and vegetativeness. Everything was put off from one day to the next; everyone was temporizing till the world settled down, the state was consolidated, and there appeared some room for maneuver. The atmosphere of wait-and-see also dominated in literature; it seemed as if Polish writers preferred not to speak more emphatically until they were certain of their national fate.

I rebelled [probable gap in the text] I refused to accept a waiting role and, seeing that such a role was imposed by the collectivity, I refused to link my fate to that of the collectivity. Some may condemn such a position, but let us agree that at times—I'm not speaking about myself—a rebel of this sort striving for unrestricted freedom is worth more to his homeland than those who meekly submit to their destiny. "Give me a place to stand and I will move the earth": I applied those words of Galileo to relations in Poland, and it occurred to me that in order to move something in Poland one needed a place to stand outside of Poland.

Outside of Poland? But where? Where could I stand?

I placed no trust in faiths, doctrines, ideologies, institutions. Thus I could stand only upon my own feet. But I was a Pole, molded by Polishness, living in Poland. And so I needed to look deeper for my "self," in the place where it was no longer Polish but simply human.

After I finished the comedy *Princess Ivona,* which was published in *Skamander* but which due to its "modernness" had no chance of finding its way onto the stage, I began work on a novel; I had no inkling that it would end up being titled *Ferdydurke.* I started this project in a strange, divided state of mind. Within me there swirled ambitions and painful grudges; I was sore and vengeful and wanted to prove myself, but at the same time common sense—which fortunately had never abandoned me—told me that I shouldn't measure my strengths according to my intentions, but rather my intentions in light of my strengths. And so I began to sketch the thing out as a regular satire, nothing more, which would permit me to make a show of my humor and perhaps—this I dreamed of—to equal Antoni Słonimski, whose jokes I admired.

Such were my horizons as I wrote the first thirty or forty pages. But a few scenes came out more powerfully, or perhaps more strangely. In them, the satire turned into a grotesquery that was utterly unrestrained, preposterous, nightmarish—an entirely different sort of thing than Słonimski's humor. I decided to maintain the whole in this spirit; I went back, started again from the beginning, and thus, slowly, there emerged a certain style that was to absorb my more essential sufferings and rebellions. I mention this because it's usually in such a way—during the process of "improving" the text to match certain more successful passages—that form is created in literature.

I worked hard—six hours a day.

I think that it was at this time I came to know Jerzy Andrzejewski, who had just brought out his first book. We met in one of the cafés, the Ipsa or the Ziemiańska. But Andrzejewski felt ill at ease at my table; between us there was too great a difference in temperament, experiences, and upbringing.

When he first joined us I turned to Otwinowski and said, "So then, Mr. Otwinowski, tell us what impression Mr. Andrzejewski makes on you."

This system of mine for bringing people together and breaking the ice didn't always work. Otwinowski was disconcerted; eventually he muttered some compliments: that Andrzejewski was intelligent, pleasant, sincere. I interrupted him and asked him to spare us the good qualities, but rather to focus on the shortcomings, which were much more interesting. I knew that this maneuver was irritating, but Andrzejewski's reaction exceeded my expectations: Instead of shrugging it off with a laugh, he scowled and stiffened, and I sensed coldness and distance between us. A sense of humor certainly wasn't his strong suit. But in this case it may have been more that he couldn't abide being made the subject of conversation. He was as ambitious as he was sensitive; his personality was in a state of perpetual threat, and everywhere he felt that people were plotting against him.

When he left, we began a serious discussion of his good and bad sides. Someone said that "he'll never succeed in being dramatic because he never stops being dramatic." Reading Andrzejewski's work in later years, I was struck by the accuracy of this observation, which at first glance seemed paradoxical. Black ceases to be black when one looks through dark glasses. Andrzejewski never seized the richness of life's colors; he was attuned to one color, one key, a minor one, and this deprived his vision of authenticity.

He had another defect that could already be seen in all his reactions: He was one of those who were incapable of walking without a cane. He couldn't take a single step without relying on an ideal, an ideology, standards, or inferred norms of behavior; he was a moralist, but not a free and, one might say, "natural" one, but one who was "principled." Without a signpost he could not move. This man truly did need God; he wasn't created for life in a world without order. But his lack of straightforwardness took its revenge on him, making his writing too rigid and even artificial, depriving it of originality.

Who knows if he would not have been a much greater writer if he hadn't left my table back then. Once again I must indicate that this is not arrogance speaking; I only mean that my world was a necessary complement to his world, and I was a natural ally in his struggle with his own stiffness. But he believed the applause that proclaimed him a "serious" artist.

*

When I met Andrzejewski he was close to Stanisław Piasecki, the editor of the weekly *Prosto z mostu,* and his group. Many young writers and poets were attracted to *Prosto z mostu,* not because they were nationalists, but because they simply couldn't come to terms with *Wiadomości Literackie,* which was edited by Grydzewski in what was called in those days a Masonic-liberal manner. Andrzejewski was one of those who need principles, guiding ideas, a closely defined moral code; he lacked the flexibility to rely on sense, instinct, ordinary goodness, and high-mindedness that doesn't arise from theory. He was already preparing himself for the role of moralist—a Catholic moralist in the deeper, perhaps Conradian style. It was no surprise that he was at odds with *Wiadomości.*

I also had my disagreements with Grydzewski and his influential weekly. I'll say frankly that in my view, though Grydzewski's intelligence was sharp and quick, it was not sufficiently penetrating or profound to have the necessary understanding of a literature as difficult as mine. In saying this I don't mean to say that my works were brilliant, only that because of their desire for newness and originality they were much harder to evaluate. Or perhaps Grydzewski wasn't to blame so much as his entourage: those various friends and confidants who whispered in his ear, telling him what was good and what was bad. If I had made friends with the Skamandrists—if I had circulated their jokes—if I'd paid visits to the editorial offices of *Wiadomości* and genuflected before Boy-Żeleński—things would no doubt have looked otherwise, since Grydzewski's entire show was run according to personal likes and dislikes. But I was galled by the commanding tone that Grydzewski assumed, especially toward us younger writers. He once telephoned me, and as it often took me some time to pick up the phone, he roared at me: "Why does one have to wait so long for you, Mr. Gombrowicz?" I replied, emphasizing every word, "I'm sorry, I was on the toilet."

Shares on the literary stock market were a political game of warring coteries, intrigues, and everything but art and literature. Someone suspected of even mild anti-semitism could not be backed by *Wiadomości;* and it was my misfortune that the hero of one of my short stories was born of a Polish father and a Jewish mother. This was enough for me to be showered with praise by Adolf Nowaczyński, a pathological Jew-hater; and Nowaczyński's praises were enough for cold winds to blow from the direction of *Wiadomości.* I was utterly innocent: In the story in question racial issues in the everyday sense of the word were of no interest to me; I had a great number of Jewish friends and had never engaged in anti-semitism. But what was the innocence of an artist when faced with the political fury of editors? As a result *Wiadomości* never properly recognized me in literature, restricting itself to "positive" but measured reviews; I imagine that Grydzewski must be kicking himself today, now that my books have acquired prestige throughout Europe.

But the lack of support from *Wiadomości* didn't send me into the arms of Piasecki. What irked me in Piasecki was not so much his nationalism or even his "fascism" as his dull-mindedness and his vulgar nature. He didn't have an ounce of art in him, and had no flair for such things; he was a politician, and one of that—for me most unpleasant—kind who operate "in culture," on the borderline between politics and art. He sought to turn writers and artists into a political force, and he actually managed to gather about himself a circle which was very second-rate yet also loud, even clamorous; that whole undertaking of Piasecki's meant the lowering of our already far from lofty position by at least one floor. He courted me too to begin with, especially because he couldn't figure out just what I was: He had never read anything of mine, and he had heard rumors that I was a free agent. But these advances ended when at his request I gave him an excerpt from *Ferdydurke* just before the book came out so he could publish it in his weekly. When he read it he was dumbfounded; he snapped his fingers and, instead of printing the extract, he declared war on me. I remember I was returning to Warsaw from Zakopane on the train one time when I noticed that the lady sitting opposite me in the compartment was engrossed in an extensive front-page article in *Prosto z mostu* entitled "Picking One's Teeth." I sensed that this was about me; when she had finished reading I asked to look at her paper, and it turned out that almost the entire issue was devoted to me; aside from this article by Piasecki, which ripped me to pieces, there were further malicious comments on the second page, a disparaging column on the third, and on the fourth I believe a letter to the editor against slander and libel. In this campaign against me, Piasecki's most powerful weapon was the nationalist-Catholic critic Jan Emil (if I remember correctly) Skiwski, of whom Słonimski used to say that his was the most noble of Polish names since it not only ended but also began with "ski." During the last war this Skiwski fell in with the Germans and wrote propaganda for them in the gutter press, because of which he had to scarper from Poland afterward; to the best of my knowledge he's living in Switzerland at present. He was a dangerous foe: one of those critics who would never amount to anything, being devoid of sensitivity or intuition, but who are highly persuasive when they lend their services to some doctrine or ideal and act as the mouthpiece for someone else's profundity and wisdom. He was by nature a teacher, a moralist, educator of the nation, and even its savior; such things are highly profitable in Poland—and thus he had a readership.

But Andrzejewski remained the apple of Piasecki's eye right up until the war: He was a Catholic, a moralist too, an educator, anti-Masonic, a fine writer, a pure-blooded Pole ... everything as it should be ... and I don't think Piasecki ever gave up on Andrzejewski, though their relations gradually became more distant. Andrzejewski, on the other hand, for tactical reasons avoided conflict with the editor of *Prosto z mostu,* but in our circles in the café he made no secret of the fact that he was filled with ever greater distaste at the methods and tricks of that group, and especially their brutal disregard for purely artistic values.

Once he even took a stand on my behalf in an incident which I'll recount not because it was significant in itself but because it was typical of my unrest at that time. I went with young Paweł Zdziechowski to the country, to his parents' property in Poznań province, and we were soon joined there by Witold Małcużyński. I spent a couple of weeks there, and was treated most hospitably. Andrzejewski, who was a friend of Paweł's, also visited. Our time was spent in conversation and music. Upon my return to Warsaw I wrote a few pieces for the *Kurier Poranny* about my Poznań interlude. But I was so filled with a strange anger, and I carried so much bitterness on the subject of country houses, beginning with my own, that I was unable to refrain from certain malicious comments.

Here I must add that according to my views of that time, a so-called social faux pas was a highly creative element in art; I believed that an artist afraid of impropriety, tastelessness, scandal, was worth little, and submission to social forms was not good for those who create form. And so, knowing full well that what I wrote was not proper, for this very reason I wrote it. Those few spiteful remarks, not addressed to anyone in particular by the way, would have disappeared without an echo, had they not been seized upon by Piasecki, who was already out to cook my goose. A note appeared in *Prosto z mostu* saying that Gombrowicz is an arrogant and impertinent fellow, because he was invited to the country by Mr. and Mrs. X and repaid them by defaming them, et cetera, et cetera. *Prosto z mostu* was not known for its subtlety of expression; the whole affair immediately became serious and most sordid. In fact, I accepted all this with philosophical calm, since I was accustomed to such things. I wrote a few conciliatory words to Mr. Zdziechowski and expressed my regrets; but in the evening, at the Zodiak café we discussed the matter more extensively and I explained to those present that, whatever my misdeed might have been in terms of ordinary decency, for me it had a deeper meaning: It was an experiment, a conscious transgression of form, and so in any case Piasecki's interpretation was false.

It was then that I first heard from Andrezejewski's lips a bitter and harsh appraisal of Piasecki's methods; he also stressed the duplicity and vileness of this politics that was invading art. I believe he was franker than he was later, when he himself was harnessed to a political yoke.

*

March 27, 1961

Have I already mentioned the visits to Zofia Nałkowska's?

Her home was one of the centers of literary life in Warsaw. Soon after the publication of my first book I was introduced to that salon, whose principal adornment was a palm tree in an immense tub, cared for with maternal solicitude by Madame Zofia, who admired the odd shapes made by nature.

Madame Zofia, the only female member of the Academy of Literature, would take a seat on the sofa and would lead the conversation like the distinguished matrons of prewar times: I was reminded of the "five o'clock teas" that my mother used to hold, or receptions at the canonesses'. But there was no question that the intelligence and refinement of this remarkable woman were reflected in the level of the conversation, and were more than adequate for coping with the truly varied elements that took part in these discussions. I often admired the skill with which this lady was able to raise a spark even from notorious recluses and stutterers, and those known for their taciturnity and their lack of polish. Her social talents broke down only with Witkiewicz: When that giant with the mien of a cunning schizophrenic came into view, Madame Zofia would cast desperate glances at her confidants; for from that moment the conversation would go to hell, and Witkacy would take the floor. That man would start to languish if he ceased even for a second to be the center of interest: It had to be either that people were speaking about him, or to him, or that he himself was speaking. He couldn't abide any other arrangement, and when at times, thanks to a mighty effort on the part of the hostess, some exchange of views was achieved on the side, Witkacy immediately began to grow so intensely bored, and to be so evidently silent, that everyone felt as if they had committed a mortal sin. And it must be added that Witkacy was not one of those who simply say what they have to say. There was nothing more contorted, bizarre, or difficult than his manner of speaking, which was calculated for effect, always on the borderline of playacting, tomfoolery, and circus tricks. It was without a doubt intelligent, but terrifyingly cold, cynical, monotonous, a kind of madness perhaps reminiscent of that contemporary clown Salvador Dali.

Fortunately he was an infrequent guest at Nałkowska's. The range of her acquaintances was extremely broad. It included the political world, especially Piłsudski's camp, with whom she was close, since the Marshal himself was a rather close friend of hers—in fact, Piłsudski once even stayed with her for a few days, during the coup I believe. She recalled her guest with great admiration, though also not without a certain frisson—on several occasions she told me about his oppressive personality, and how it overwhelmed all those around him. She would say in surprise: "When he was here I would walk about on tiptoe in my own apartment; even in the furthest room I didn't dare speak loudly, though I was well aware he couldn't hear me."

Aside from Piłsudski's people, and government and political circles, there was of course literature and art. Karol Szymanowski, for instance, who regrettably did not find my little book of stories entirely to his liking; but above all women, whose relations with Nałkowska were rather complicated and, I might say, perverse: for she was not unduly fond of them, preferring male society, while on the other hand she had a sense of female solidarity, which obliged her to "spread her sheltering wings," as Breza maliciously put it.

The most onerous feature of Madame Zofia's salon, however, were some strange characters, for the most part gray and terribly inconspicuous, neither flesh, fish, nor good red herring, occasionally real oddballs, who had come from goodness knows where. A good few of them, I suspect, the elegant hostess owed to Bogusław Kuczyński, a young man of perhaps twenty-five who was a friend of hers. Kuczyński was a beginning author and had published a book entitled *Women on the Way,* which was so economical and severe in its language that it couldn't count on a wide readership. But it was precisely such works, strange, marginal, breaking out of norms, that most attracted Nałkowska's lively intellect. She was probably also rather attracted by Kuczyński himself, a handsome young fellow, though extremely untalkative, of whom someone coined the expression that "it's as if he were gagged." He was touchy, nervous, dramatic, and looked like a true martyr. He spoke quietly, elaborately, and with difficulty, as if tormented by the fact that he was unable to express his deepest inner truth. He was perpetually on edge and constantly "experiencing" something, though it was never clear what.

It was Bogusław the Gagged, who was a friend of mine and of the other young folk, that dragged along to Madame Zofia's a mixed bunch of cranks as if just in case . . . who knew, maybe something would come of them. And it was this that Nałkowska reveled in most of all—in sniffing out talent, unearthing something of value, even of the kind you need a magnifying glass to see. She would be brought a manuscript by some poet no one had ever heard of, and three days later he was being discussed over tea. And often her knack for discovering the new brought results: It was she who discovered Schulz, promoted Rudnicki and Breza, supported Piętak, nor was I refused her aid and advice. It was hardly surprising that young folk were drawn to her. She in turn was drawn to young people; she was amazingly vital for her age, and she aroused the envy of other women, who would say sneeringly, "Literature conserves . . ."

Was she a snob? That was a charge that stuck to her; but I personally was never convinced by the idea of her alleged snobbery. She liked receiving guests; she liked elegance, and she herself was an elegant and even worldly woman. And these qualities, so ordinary in Paris, became almost indecent and provocative in certain circles in Warsaw. And I suspect that if she'd been less of a "leftist" she would not have been accused so readily of snobbery—for it was only against the background of her leftism that Madame Zofia's exquisite manners stood out particularly glaringly. In general it must be said that this woman belonged neither in Warsaw nor in Poland; her place was Paris, or in any case western Europe.

This was a point of especial interest to me—for I too felt out of place in Poland, and I leaned toward Europe with all my being. But in a short time I realized that Nałkowska's Europe was not my Europe. I wasn't unduly fond of her books . . . and there arose a situation that was even a little deceitful—not for the first time, alas, and not with her alone—since I couldn't reciprocate her abundant, praiseful interest with even a single more enthusiastic word. Because when it came down to it, I could not abide such Europeans as Nałkowska, who acquired Europe's *savoir vivre* yet avoided any essential confrontation with the West. In my understanding this was an imitation of Europe, and not genuine contact with it.

If Nałkowska had been more strongly, more painfully in touch with the realities of Poland . . . If she'd followed in the footsteps of Chopin, who conquered Europe with his Polishness, that is, with his own personal authentic reality . . . But she felt closer to Szymanowski, who, despite his great talent, never managed to find his own personal, and thus national, reality—he exploited it esthetically, but he never conquered it spiritually. And thus, Nałkowska was more Europe's ambassador in Poland than Poland's representative in Europe, and in my view this was not the best method for transforming oneself into a genuine European.

I remember one walk I took with her in the Łazienki Park. We strolled along the autumnal paths and finally sat down on a bench. She was enraptured at the sight of a tree that was a few yards from us. It was one of those cold yet passionate exaltations that she experienced with stones, fish, plants. It started with various exclamations such as, "Just look at that line . . . the embodiment of slenderness," and it ended in comparisons that almost belonged in the salon: "My, that tree is stylish! It's like a fine lady!" For some reason I was angry with her—perhaps I'd had enough of these urbanities of hers—and in the end I said, not without a dose of sarcasm, "I see you're investing your entire soul in that tree!" Instead of being offended, she grew melancholy and replied, "It's true; in my case beauty not only makes my life harder, it also makes it harder for me to find my relation to life."

Such words may well encapsulate the drama of this exceptional woman.

*

On Zofia Nałkowska's name day her apartment on Marszałkowska Street, near Unii Lubelskiej Square, was always filled with massive numbers of guests. In 1935, on that day of St. Sophia (or perhaps a day close to it), a huge crowd had gathered—colonels, generals, ministers, editors, writers, members of parliament, painters, the theater world—one could hardly squeeze through the throng.

The party was just reaching its climax when suddenly something happened. I was unable at first to figure out the reason for this abrupt yet so pronounced change; around me, by the buffet, people were conversing with glasses and small plates in their hands. But in the general hum of conversation something seemed to have broken down.

All at once I saw some woman writer—maybe Szelburg-Zarembina, or perhaps Melcer-Rutkowska—crying as she left the drawing room. Her face was bathed in tears. What was it? Could someone have insulted her?

Then two more women left, sobbing loudly, followed by several men wearing dramatic expressions. And all around, silence began to take the place of the clamor of the reception. Again a number of people moved toward the door, hurriedly donning their coats.

At last I understood: Piłsudski. It had been known for several days that his condition was serious.

By now everyone was leaving, exchanging quiet and hurried goodbyes; and since the presidential palace was close by, Madame Zofia's guests ran off in that direction. I followed them, with Adolf Rudnicki and a few others. Scarcely two or three cars stood in front of the palace, and there was only a handful of people waiting outside the gates—the news had not yet spread around the city, and we were among the first to have heard. The white façade of the Belweder palace, clearly visible in the light of the street lamps, was mysterious and silent.

All at once a procession of Cadillacs began to drive into the court-yard—it was the government, led by Prime Minister Składkowski, reporting to the Marshal for the last time.

In today's tempestuous era everyone has had their share of historic moments, myself included. After all, I'd been present at the end of the First World War, the rebirth of Poland, the Battle for Warsaw, the May Coup, and so on. But at such times, I always felt something like a re-volt against history, and couldn't reconcile myself to the fact that I was nothing, a piece of straw blown in the wind, and that everything was taking place outside of me. This can probably be ascribed to my fierce individualism, which is beyond my control, since I was born with it and will die with it. I would be lying if I claimed that the Mar-shal's death did not distress me profoundly. With him a certain pe-riod of our existence also died; the country, deprived of his firm hand, was stepping into an Unknown bristling with perils. But seeing the cream of the Polish intelligentsia gathered in front of the Belweder like a covey of partridges, humble, trembling, terrified, immobilized, as if it weren't a man who had died but a superman, irritated me in a manner as unexpected as it was acute. By all means, let the military, the civil servants, the ordinary citizens react like this . . . but intellec-tuals, philosophers, artists? Where was their strength, their maturity? Were they not even slightly more stable than those others, the subor-dinates? Were they too expecting someone to take care of them and lead them—that someone higher and more powerful would look after the machine in which they were no more than little cogs?

I gazed in exasperation at the pale faces of some of my fellow writ-ers and said aloud to no one in particular, "What nice cars!"

It isn't hard to imagine the effect. The more kindly disposed ex-plained to those less sympathetic that I was a bit crazy and a bit of an actor, that it was a pose, that I was pretending to be cynical and tact-less. Yet I wasn't so crazy in those days, and maybe Piłsudski was not so offended at my insubordination as he lay on his catafalque . . . he who did indeed like obedience, but also valued dignity, freedom, and pride in Poles. It was just that at the time I was incapable of explaining these outbursts of mine, which were colored more by idealism than cynicism. I was a beginning writer who had carved out his own genre of imaginative prose but did not yet know how to write simply and accessibly about what pained him and troubled him.

Piłsudski! It's not my place to evaluate his policies—though I'm inclined to think that even if Poland had been led at the time by Churchill, or Mussolini, or even Napoleon and Talleyrand together, they would not have been able to accomplish much more, since the potential of Polish politics was hugely restricted by the geographical location of this small country in the convulsive heart of a Europe already sick with all the illnesses that were soon to break out. Piłsudski did whatever could be done, in whatever way it could be done; and his realism, boldness, and courage stood in sharp contrast to the cowardly pacifism of the over-smart bourgeoisie of France or England with their Briand, their League of Nations, and their Locarno. As an artist, I was enthralled and entertained by the Marshal's style— that entire characteristic grand, delectable, colorful manner of his, and his unmistakable, delectable greatness. It was at the same time both perfectly Polish and utterly his own. We writers often spent hours discussing this astounding figure, relishing it and attempting to decipher its secrets. Yet in these conversations sentiment prevailed, and often respect made analysis impossible; at such times Piłsudski's greatness almost always remained beyond question, like something that has been established once and for all.

"You talk about him as if he'd been 'conferred' upon you," I once said. "As if History had given you the gift of a great man. And since they say one shouldn't look a gift horse in the mouth, you don't ask where this greatness of his comes from and why."

And indeed, in the attitude of Polish intellectuals toward Piłsudski there was a great deal of convention and even clichés. It was common knowledge that Poland sometimes had great individuals; well then, he was one of them and that was all there was to it. But such alacrity in adoration and obedience was not becoming in the elite of the nation. What's appropriate for a soldier is not always recommended for an intellectual. The chair of the Cabinet, Sławoj, standing stiffly to attention before the Marshal, really did not represent the highest accomplishments of Polish reason. And that romantic, sentimental, naive helplessness of the Polish intelligentsia in relation to Piłsudski harmed him himself—for Piłsudski was the first victim of his own legend, and Piłsudski may never have impressed anyone as much as he impressed himself.

Naturally I'm not forgetting that public debate on this issue was impossible at the time, not so much because of the reaction of the authorities, but because the Marshal had admirers who were as ardent as they were ready for a scrap. True, I wasn't always fully aware of these taboos. It was thanks to Nałkowska that before it was too late I removed a humorous poem from *Ferdydurke* that parodied the legions' song "The First Brigade." She raised the roof: "Have you gone mad?! This is asking for trouble." Luckily the text had not yet been sent to the printer's, so there was still time to patch the passage over without difficulty. But, though anything that concerned the legend of Piłsudski and the legions was beyond the pale of free commentary in the press or in books, in conversation one could say whatever one liked.

This freedom, however, was not taken advantage of in the literary world. Neither the Skamandrists, who were after all so quick to poke fun, nor critics like Boy-Żeleński or Irzykowski, nor the left, nor even the circles associated with the *Kurier Warszawski,* nor the right-wing national democrats led by Nowaczyński. On various occasions the Marshal was attacked for one or another aspect of his policies; but in my experience it never happened that his very greatness itself was subject to discussion and analysis in those last years of his rule. The catchword that "Poland has had great men and the great man of Poland is now Piłsudski" had taken root even in the subconscious of his enemies.

I won't deny that he may well have been great. For me it was not his greatness that chafed, but the smallness of those who submitted to it so eagerly. I had nothing whatsoever against the masses for following him blindly, but I was perturbed by the ease with which the leading classes of society renounced their right to criticism and skepticism, to—and this is the appropriate word—scrutiny.

*

April 27, 1961

Something should also be said about the women of those distant times. My mother and sister were virtuous believers, "women of principle" as the phrase was then, and thus the representatives of the fair sex who visited our home were known more for their virtues than their flirtatiousness—those various girlfriends of my sister, Rena, from the Society of Landed Ladies and the Catholic Mission, who mostly devoted themselves to an assortment of philanthropic activities and were most uninterested in coquetry. My brothers, who were older than I was, felt wronged, because normally a sister's friends constitute natural prey for her brothers; and so they had a rather hostile and malicious attitude to these friends and to the "principles" they worshipped.

Yet what a difference there was between my mother's faith and my sister's—as if they were two separate languages! My mother's Catholicism was spontaneous, natural, almost rash in its naturalness—it was the air that she breathed without being aware of it and without any effort. True, she liked to broach various theological issues, but she did so with an indolence that proved she was quite unprepared for it. Here the ideal was manifest in a certain way of being, and my mother was a devout Catholic just as she was a Pole and a member of the landed gentry.

My sister, on the other hand, was difficult in her faith, intent, concentrated; it was what we would call today an "existential" Catholicism that showed how very difficult life had become over the course of a single generation. It was already a modern Catholicism. There is no doubt, incidentally, that she had the strongest character of all of us. Besides, she was powerfully drawn to logic, precision, scientific objectivity, and it was not for nothing that she had studied mathematics. Her faith too was as much reasoned as it was emotional, but it was almost completely devoid of joy, at least the kind that manifests itself easily on the outside; and it was almost dramatic in its stubbornness. Often, observing those two women, I would reflect with a certain disquiet on the kind of severity and coldness which became characteristic of our generation—and which I perceived also in myself and my literary and nonliterary peers. These were signs in heaven and earth that announced the birth of new and so much tougher times.

I don't mean to say by this that all those Catholic women of the new kind were equally categorical and profound; quite the opposite, they included a considerable mixture of modern intellectualism with the former ease, and boundaries were not strictly set; and yet amongst them there appeared a gravity that broke through the platitudes they had inherited. It was just that at times the combination of these elements created truly comic effects, which we brothers greeted with gales of laughter. For it must be confessed that that still inept gravity, that ardor which could not express itself because it was too timid and mute, or which sometimes resorted to bombast—all this sometimes prompted resistance and mockery, and I believe that many a man was alienated from the church by precisely this new emerging style of female Catholicism.

We made fun of these "excesses" in the name of common sense and realism, and often mocked their virtue in exactly the way the Marxists would have done—in other words, demonstrating that it was the fruit of bourgeois pampering, of the comforts that the upper social spheres provide. Such reproaches rarely made any impact on my mother; she rejected them out of hand as originating from a spirit of unbelief and malice—but in young ladies of my sister's type they found an unexpectedly strong resonance. These young women already knew that beyond "their" world was concealed another, a much fouler reality that it would not be possible to avoid. Their delicacy desperately sought some spiritual fortification which would enable them to face this sinister reality; like well-mannered maidens, they continued to try not to notice certain "dirty facts of life," but they were already mobilizing their deepest reserves to be able to face them head on, and not to be taken by surprise when the time came to do so.

While older women could see nothing whatsoever wrong with their material wealth, the younger ladies from "good homes" were perpetually accompanied by feelings of guilt. "It's not my fault I was born into well-off circles," my sister would defend herself. "We all have to live wherever God has placed us. But my life ought not to be easier than other, less fortunate lives; in any case I ought to live for those other lives. It's not a matter of getting rid of my possessions, or the values to which a better education gave me access, but of enabling others to have access to them."

And, faithful to her mathematical inclinations, she would add, "Tell me, is that not logical?"

She remained true to this logic of hers throughout her life. She was hard-working, conscientious, scrupulous, and devoted to charitable work; she strove to maximize the effectiveness of what she did and was modest and quiet as she went about it.

But these more modern Catholic women, for the most part young, were encumbered by the ballast of tradition, of various already outdated conventions, the phraseology of their mothers and aunts, against which they did not wish to rebel too much. These older ladies were often quite unbearable in their naive and oh-so-comfortable grandiloquence. The myth of the Polish woman, guardian of the domestic hearth, representative of the spirit, called upon to inspire the man with said spirit—this myth, created by the literature of Rodziewiczówna and her ilk, was, like anything of poor quality, deeply pernicious. And such a lofty program was far from difficult to implement: The husband earned money or gathered the profits from his estates, and his wife was the "guardian" of ideals that ought not to be looked in the mouth since they were a gift from their esteemed parents and grandparents. How many female guardians and priestesses have I known! They were individuals filled with the best intentions, striving to bring up their husband and children as best as possible, but they were lazy and had no clue about anything, convinced that a knowledge of the ten commandments was all the wisdom they needed. Alas, it became impossible to have any real educative influence when one had not kept up with intellectual and cultural advancements. Yet it was not this that most rankled with younger people, but rather the ever more visible falseness of their position, their tone.

Every writer, even one just beginning, becomes something of a counselor and confessor. A student I knew once admitted to me that he had thought about killing his mother.

"But you were always devoted to her; you loved her," I observed.

"I don't deny it," he replied, sipping his coffee in the small café where we were talking, "but at the same time I can't stand her. You have no idea how she annoys me! I'm not at all fond of my father, but at least he's a regular fellow, like everyone else, and doesn't put on airs. But my mother! She's an actress of the worst kind: noble, steadfast, suffering. She does nothing but declaim! It's true that that was exactly why I respected her, even worshipped her; but now it's exactly why I want to strike her!"

There were many such toxins in these God-fearing families, which incidentally shows how society was rapidly maturing. Poland at that time was a land of dying styles, forms which were being put to death like sick animals . . . but these formal dissonances were exactly what I was looking for while I was writing *Ferdydurke!* It's not always that the vengefulness of the new generation takes on such a dramatic shape. One of my friends had a bone to pick with one of his aunts, who as guardian and foster mother had disapproved loudly of his engagement with a young lady who wasn't "suitable" enough. My friend found himself a good-looking streetwalker, taught her so-called salon manners in the course of a few lessons, and then took her under an assumed name to his aunt's salon. The courtesan apparently behaved magnificently, drinking her tea and eating her petits fours beyond reproach; but it turned out that she had too many acquaintances amongst the gentlemen present. This led to consternation, the consternation to panic, and the panic to scandal, resulting in the ejection not only of the poor woman of the night, but of my friend too.

*

I rarely met with Boy-Żeleński. From time to time I would attend his teas, and I can't say I enjoyed them: the crowd, the tea-drinking standing up, and the conversation that was so ephemeral you began a sentence with one person and ended it with another. The host himself was too much in demand and constantly being greeted for him to spend much time with anyone.

I had little contact with the women who surrounded him, mostly because this secondhand, feminized Boyism I found not only not attractive, but actually repellent. These were either older women writers who constituted a kind of female general staff of the master, or pretty young women, sometimes actresses or poets, often quite simply girls who were drawn to an environment in which their beauty could exist in a way that was easier and more productive, and without fear. But, strange to relate, in the immediate orbit of Boy-Żeleński the charms of these women seeking an "easier life" were much less alluring; there was something deliberate, something theoretical about them, and this overly stereotypical emancipation was sometimes vexsome.

I must admit, however, that this man achieved great things as far as the normalization of Polish women was concerned. I use the term *normalization* to refer to the situation that had arisen. I've already mentioned the extent to which the older generation of women of the intelligentsia was still burdened by the cheap phraseology that the traditions and literature of the preceding period had fed them— these ladies were almost always a little over the top, if not in one thing then another, always inclined to pursue some "mission" and to speak in the name of "higher principles." Of course, there would be nothing wrong in all this, were it not for the fact that a lack of intellectual sophistication and a surfeit of naivety rendered them virtually childlike in this sublime role. And as concerns their daughters, who were much better at controlling themselves and who frequently succeeded in deepening their Catholicism, this profound experience of faith turned out badly only in those whose natures were specially designed for it. An ordinary young woman, who didn't shun entertainment or flirtation and wished to find a husband, tended to feel uncomfortable in such an outsized suit of armor; she would lose her sense of proportion and fail to understand what was expected of her and what her obligations were. To this would be added the glaring discrepancy between the atmosphere of science classes at university or school, where liberalism reigned, and the spirit of severity in which she was immersed at home.

This disequilibrium in women was a great problem for us young people. No one knew what sort of woman he would encounter and what torments he'd have to go through with her. It would seem, for example, that when a girl began to gaze tenderly and playfully at her sweetheart, the latter was entitled to look forward to various pleasant things. But it happened to me—and I think not to me alone—that a certain good-looking blonde flirted with me not to seduce me but for my moral edification! I was twenty-some years old then; we met several times, and she treated me so tenderly that in the end I asked her out on a date.

"Very well," she whispered, blushing, "but no one can see us!"

I screwed up my courage and suggested that she come to my place. She went pale, then blushed, but agreed.

Yet when she appeared at the appointed time, she didn't take off her coat and hat.

"You probably imagine goodness knows what about me! But I'm not like that. I've come to have a serious talk with you. I want to help you; I can see that you're in pain."

And there began a lecture explaining that the road I had taken was not the right one, that she wanted to show me the light, that I lacked ideals, and so on and so forth. I thought to myself that she could have done without this kind of introduction; but to me it smacked of the worst kind of falsehood, and I decided to stick it out in the hope that we'd soon switch to another subject. Nothing of the sort! The lessons in idealism went on and on, and when in the end I asked her if she didn't think she had misled me, she took offense.

"Who do you take me for! Yes, I was interested in you, but only because you've gone astray!"

This exasperating combination of old and new elements, of the modern ease of manner and principles, eroticism and idealism, sex and soul, was a common phenomenon. Polish women are undoubtedly an outstanding example of womankind: intelligent, bold, vigorous, enterprising—but it's precisely this that inclines them to take command. They want to guide their man, educate him, save him, ennoble him. . . . He'll always remain something of a child for them. As for me, in moral matters I still sometimes received those teachings meekly, though deep down I was convinced that in this too I knew better than they did—but when they began opening my soul to beauty and uttering platitudes about art, the writer in me would awake and I'd take a stand.

"For the love of God," I once said to one such female esthete, "just think about yourself a little! You read virtually nothing. You have no notion of music or painting: You can't tell Beethoven from Mozart, Brahms from Bach, or Titian from Velasquez; you've barely looked at Shakespeare and Goethe—so what are you talking about? Your whole life indicates that you don't like art and don't understand it.

Why would you decide to teach someone like me who is immersed in it?"

She answered calmly as anything, "Yes, but you lack ideals and principles."

Well! To that there was no reply. Principles and ideals took the place of hard work, passion, and expert knowledge. Such arrogance, which absolved one of the need for hard work, was often found amongst those Catholic women, who were convinced they "knew better," though many a priest combated it by observing correctly that faith ought not to be an encouragement to pride or idleness.

These few examples are enough to make it clear why I charge a considerable percentage of the women of that time with a lack of balance. They were like an untuned musical instrument; they lacked naturalness and a sense of perspective in word and deed. And it was here, in my view, that Boy-Żeleński's journalism was truly fruitful—independently of the shocking and even scandalous aspect it possessed for many respectable older and younger ladies, it was nevertheless a school of humor, of a sense of realism, of a modern way of coexistence. Boy-Żeleński's common sense somehow managed to infect even those who regarded him as a demon and, worse, a Mason; it filtered down through his lady friends and acquaintances all the way to the most conservative circles, and it gradually changed women's ways of being, that form to which I attach such importance, seeing in it as I do the key to so many aches and the secret to so many sicknesses. Through their struggles with him, Boy-Żeleński's staunchest female opponents became freer, more flexible, and as it were more capable.

A few years before the war, in Zakopane I once took a trip to Hala Gąsienicowa with a group of ladies who had just returned to Poland after living abroad for several years. Many things irritated them, and soon our conversation was teeming with anecdotes and comments illustrating the lack of refinement of Polish women, their awkwardness, their failings, their ineptitude, especially toward men. In this way we reached the hostel on Hala, where there was a small group of sixteen- and seventeen-year-old girls—a school outing under the supervision of a few female teachers.

Just at that time there appeared an outing of male students from some technical school in Kraków. The encounter of these young people took place so smoothly, without any discord caused by excessive prudery or unruliness—welcoming smiles and friendly greetings materialized so readily and were so engaging—that we in our corner had to confess this new crop was quite different, as if liberated from the hell of dissonances. A very great deal had changed—gone were entire registers of affectation, exaggeration, airs and graces, that whole convulsiveness marking the older generation. Was this Boy-Żeleński's work? Probably so, but only to a small degree. Something more powerful—the spirit of the times itself—played the biggest part.

*

May 29, 1961

A certain philosopher, I forget exactly who, classified nations into those that have a feminine culture and those in which masculine culture predominates. This traveler—now I remember, it was a German thinker by the name of Keyserling, who had visited many countries and had become a great expert in national psychology—used to say that determining which cultural group, the masculine or the feminine, a given nation belongs to is the easiest thing in the world. One simply has to observe whose interests are better protected by the customs, laws, and institutions of that nation—those of the man, or those of the woman.

If mores are strict; if a young woman is under the control of her parents; if, in order to go for a walk with the girl you adore, you first have to declare yourself as a suitor, and even then Mama and Papa tread on your heels; if your young man's ardors can find no outlet, and everything is so masterfully arranged that you feel as if an invisible hand has seized you by the scruff of the neck and is dragging you toward the altar; and if in addition your income and its stability has become a matter of public discussion as the safeguard of hearth and home—then there's no doubt about it: You are in a country that is in the hands of women and is organized with a view to matrimony.

If, on the other hand, a young bachelor has an easy life; if public opinion is forbearing, laws lenient, and only those men marry who truly feel called upon to do so—then masculine erotic culture is dominant.

Thus, Poland between the wars was for me a country slowly changing its erotic culture from the feminine to the masculine.

I may be wrong—it's very difficult to make such sweeping judgments about Poland, if only because of the chasm that separates the common people from the intelligentsia—these were always two worlds apart. But in any case the intelligentsia, especially its artistic and intellectual branch, which I knew best, from year to year clearly revealed the growing ascendancy of the man. Ha—it wasn't just the women artists and writers, but schoolgirls as well! I became convinced of this at first hand when, not long before the war, the girls of the sixth or seventh grade of the Queen Jadwiga Grammar School invited me to a school ball. I was asked because they had, on their own initiative, prepared a performance of my short story "Filidor's Child Within," which they'd adapted for the stage, and the ball was held to mark this event. It took place in the villa of one of their number somewhere in Okęcie. When I arrived I found a living room filled with sixteen- and seventeen-year-old girls and their various boyfriends and admirers; the element of parents, aunts, and so on had been completely eliminated, leaving the young people in charge. Well then! I've found myself at all kinds of strange and spirited parties, but I had never encountered anything like this initiation into fun, vodka, and extravagance.

It started off rather dull and awkward: some desultory conversations, with intermittent laughter. I'd already begun to figure out how I might sneak away, when suddenly someone opened the door to the next room, where there was a buffet, and everyone gradually began to gather around a table bearing various alcoholic drinks. From what followed I recall the impression of an abrupt crescendo, a rapidly growing buzz, rising to the dimensions of a roar—these young people had flung themselves on the vodka. Within five minutes we were all tipsy; I've never seen so many people get drunk together so instantly, as if on command. And I of course was among them, and afterward I don't remember very clearly what happened, though I have vague memories of riding a motorcycle and climbing a tree.

Such parties testified to the marked "militarization" of young ladies' ways—I call it this since it was the style of the young people from the military schools, the style of the military life. This unruliness amongst minors, which so scandalized their elders, had at the time—at least in the closing years of the period—its own dramatic meaning: war. Its shadow lay on everything; its ominous proximity whispered that life should be enjoyed while it could, before it was overly mixed with death. These teenage girls of the last years before the war had something of the scorn for convention that characterized the young people who a couple of years later were fighting on the streets of Warsaw. "We're living as if we were about to die," an inebriated Świątek Karpiński once shouted in my ear at some booze-up; and that reflected the atmosphere hanging over Poland even more than over Europe as a whole.

And so if the generation that entered the lists immediately after the First World War was bathed in the great revolution of mores the war had given birth to, the next generation already felt the breath of the new cataclysm—and thus, between two wars young people moved ever further from the thought of marriage, family, or professional work, and entered ever more into the orbit of romance and danger.

As far as this increasing ease of manners is concerned, the difference between us and the West was, I think, that in those countries, which despite everything gave people a greater sense of security, it was more rational, a logical development, whereas in Poland it was darker, more intuitive and more dramatic. Young people in England read Wells and criticized old conceptions in the name of a new scientific, atheistic worldview that gave women the right to free love; in Poland things happened as it were by themselves, because even adolescents out of range of the official rhetoric of the great powers could read the obscure signs of the coming tragedy. Boy-Żeleński at most provided only a small few with a rational foundation; the rest adhered to the new ways not for any reason and not because they were influenced by Hitler's or Stalin's theories, but because they were simply afraid of Hitler and Stalin.

As far as I could tell from my restricted point of view, there was no shortage of Polish women whom the switch from feminine to masculine erotic culture suited very well. They felt comfortable within it, and didn't fear it in the slightest. Polish women are not excessively womanly. On the contrary, they have a good few masculine qualities: Their courage, energy, self-reliance, resourcefulness, their ambition, their desire to lead, their rich mental life and intellectual interests mean that they are far from resembling the "little woman" type often found amongst the Spanish, the Italians, and also frequently the Germans. There can be no question that this category of Polish female was stifled by the narrow role the old style of interaction with men imposed upon them. As I observed older women brought up in the former school, I had a strange impression. They seemed shocked and embarrassed, and they blushed as they recounted what their daughters got up to; yet at the same time it was as if, deep down, in secret, they actually liked it, and it was even apparent that in some way they themselves were living vicariously through their children's freedom, of which they disapproved.

But I repeat that I do not wish to generalize; I'm only recounting what I observed from my own perspective. And it was a narrow perspective: It included mostly "society" women and those from the artistic world, whereas I had no contact with legions of women from other intellectual and social spheres. I was made plainly aware of this myself in Zakopane once when I made the rather stormy acquaintance of a group of professors from the Jagiellonian University in Kraków who were staying in the same guesthouse that I was. I immediately got into an argument with these professors, and so effectively that one eminent historian seized hold of a chair to hurl at me, so upset was he by my foolish gibes; yet on the other hand I became friends with their children, who were mostly entering upon scientific careers and were studying chemistry, biology, and such subjects. These likable girls and intelligent boys introduced me in Kraków to a sizable crowd of creatures like themselves. These were young ladies who already resembled men in many ways, yet in some way also recalled the women of my mother's generation, perhaps because they were so self-possessed—yes, they were not thrill-seekers but composed, disciplined women who in some strange way seemed God-fearing, though they were often at odds with the church. But they belonged to a different church—that of science. They submitted to its rigors and from it derived virtue.

*

I personally never knew how to deal with them—I'm talking about women—and with them I always behaved exactly as I should not have. In other words I was uncouth, fantastical, aggressive, ironic, unstable. Of course, much of this was due to my various complexes and inhibitions, but I also owe a lot of it to unpleasant experiences, and the fact that I'd been stung so many times.

In *Ferdydurke,* the novel I wrote when I was nearing thirty and which was my settling of accounts with the world, there's a passage about "genteel aunts," whom I regard as an even worse plague than ordinary family aunts. These genteel aunts were a real nuisance. If I remember Nałkowska with gratitude, it's because she was one of the very few women writers who didn't treat me with auntlike indulgence from the heights of her auntlike knowledge of literature. I give a genuine sigh at the thought of the level-headed, penetrating intelligence of that exceptional lady. Others usually regarded me either as an obstreperous little boy, or as a demon, or most often as a poseur who was trying to impress with a forced originality. What was I to do? Explain? Clarify? There wouldn't have been any point: They would have understood little. These were women who at a pinch could appreciate literature that was already established, valued, and catalogued, but they were utterly helpless when faced with something that deviated from the norm. I took my revenge on them by turning myself into a madman and acting the fool as much as possible, but deep down I hated those indulgent and arrogant matrons, leaders, teachers, and—alas, it often happened—reviewers.

Just as Polish poetry of the time was dominated by men, so the women took over Polish prose. Truly exceptional writers like Schulz or Witkiewicz were considered eccentrics; Kaden-Bandrowski was ever less important; whereas Dąbrowska, Nałkowska, Kossak-Szczucka, Kuncewiczowa, Krzywicka, Naglerowa, or Gojawiczyńska were the providers of novels discussed high and wide in the press and popular with readers. It was not at all bad work, and there sometimes appeared books of great value; but this feminization of Polish prose lent it too much softness, kind-heartedness, mildness, and indistinctness, depriving it of qualities such as imagination, boldness, and strength. At a certain point I rebelled and came to the conclusion that femininity in literature had to be exterminated.

Światek Karpiński, the poet, had found a philanthropist prepared to put a considerable sum of money into an as yet chimerical project involving the creation of a new literary journal in which younger folk could find a voice. In Karpiński's conception, this little publication would in fact be a private organ for six young writers; each of them would be the independent editor of one section assigned to them.

This idea appealed to me very much, and when Światek asked what I intended to include on my page, I replied, "I'm going to fight for myself; I'm going to deal with my enemies!"

"Which ones?" he asked with interest.

"The women," I snarled.

He look at me admiringly.

"You know, that's excellent! I mean, the fact that such a good idea should have occurred to you too. I was actually also thinking of using my page to settle accounts with a few of the ladies . . . for example, the ones who left me for Minio."

As can be seen, this illustrious publication very nearly became a venue for the settling of erotic scores by Światek and his dipsomaniac pals; fortunately the philanthropist failed to come through and nothing came of it all. And I never found out if the women in literature really were my enemy, and whether I was right to hold anything against them and the femininity of literature. For we find out if our resentments are justified only when we begin to fight for them.

Nor did I have any particular success with ordinary ladies and girls who had nothing to do with the intellect. What was worse, it was precisely young ladies of this kind that I most liked—good-looking, healthy women with whom there was no need to talk about art, who in themselves were beauty and grace. Alas! How many disappointments, how many painful misunderstandings arose from those perverse tendencies of mine . . . perverse, because instead of staying close to those with whom I had a great deal in common, and who looked favorably on my intelligence and my artistic accomplishments, I chased after women to whom my reality was foreign, and who understood little or nothing of it all. True, my dual character lent itself to deception—my appearance was more that of a young member of the landed gentry than of a frequenter of cafés and an avant-garde writer; I played tennis rather well; I was knowledgeable about genealogy; I felt entirely comfortable in provincial company, and when I visited my various cousins deep in the country I often had lively conversations with them lasting into the night. And so it was only after a certain time that those innocent, charming young ladies realized that I was taking advantage of their trustfulness, that I was not what I claimed to be, and that in me there was something different, odd, perhaps even dangerous. And I too only understood after some time that nothing would come of amours based upon dissimulation.

And indeed nothing did come of any of it. These amours would end painfully when the girl discovered that, though I was enchanted by her, I wouldn't allow her to get close to me—I was always hermetic, devoted to my own matters, and never frank or open even for a moment. And I could not be otherwise with them, for it would have been easier for them to understand, for example, the nature of a crocodile than my nature, formed by influences and factors about which they knew nothing.

At least I had enough integrity never to present myself as a candidate for marriage; quite the opposite, I would give them to understand from the beginning that I'd no desire to wed.

In the end these constantly repeated failures attracted the attention both of my friends and my enemies. Tadeusz Breza telephoned me one day.

"You have to come round, there's something I have to show you."

This "something" turned out to be a certain young actress who was just starting her career but who was already well known. She was beautiful, brimming with health, pleasant, and at the same time fond of reading and familiar with art. Tadeusz imagined that this time he'd found for me an ideal combination of body and soul, culture and nature. Far from it! The fact that she appeared on the stage, that she allowed herself to be stared at, that she had what was effectively a professional attitude toward her own grace and charms, meant that I wasn't interested in the slightest.

Janusz Minkiewicz, known universally as Minio and by me as Gminio, who was famed for his conquests in the Warsaw demimonde, often took his revenge for various sarcastic remarks of mine (for I was not overly fond of him) by suggesting that I was motivated by envy.

"I'm going home now," he would say coolly and matter-of-factly, "because Lala's supposed to call me. At five I'm meeting Cela, and at 11 I'm up for some fun with Fila. Bye now."

He would leave, convinced that I was turning green with envy. But I didn't envy him. Women who could be interested in that rather feline, indolent poet could be of no interest to me, by the simple fact that they were interested in him.

In this domain I was like those gourmets who accept only the simplest dishes but insist on the highest quality. No mayonnaise, dressing, herbs, pepper, nothing prepared or complicated—wholemeal bread, but of the most delicious kind, fresh, luscious fruit straight from the tree, spring water . . . very well, but are such wonderful things meant for cripples like myself? I often encountered them in the common people, those at the lowest level of culture, and at such times I was seized with delight, as if I'd finally found something worthy of admiration in humanity; but I stopped at that silent admiration, without even attempting to reach for that which was loftier than myself.

*

June 23, 1961

I rarely ever spent any time in nightclubs. Alcohol didn't particularly entice me, dancing even less so, and those who frequented such places—both the women and the men—I found uninteresting. Also, this golden life against the backdrop of Warsaw's poverty was too grating for me—I sometimes detected hatred in the eyes of the laborers mending the road in the early morning as we were leaving the Adria in our furs and hailing a cab. True, if one of those workers could have seen our empty pockets and, even more, our empty stomachs, he would quickly have realized that those orgies of ours were not so orgiastic after all. But appearances stared one in the face—here he was, at work in the cold, and there the bourgeoisie were leaving their party in the company of young women.

I suspect that in postwar Poland there was more appearance of wrongs and injustice than actual "social exploitation." The distance between a count, old Lithuanian landowner, master, industrialist, or member of the intelligentsia on the one hand, and a worker on the other, looked immense. In reality even that landowner, industrialist, or count barely had two pennies to rub together and couldn't afford the most basic necessities. Appearances were still loud and proud: the doffing of caps, the use of titles, servants—but truth to tell, no one was in clover, and everyone was wondering how to make ends meet on one's own scale. It also sometimes happened that the greater one's wealth, the worse off one ended up being. My paltry intellectual's income still allowed me to travel abroad when I felt like it, whereas various landowning uncles of mine had to sit tight where they were, keeping an eye on taxes and expenditures and chasing around after loans.

Nor did those ill-famed dance clubs abound in luxury; at most of the tables the customers strove to consume as little as possible and from a financial point of view one could sense that the atmosphere was rather ascetic. If I did happen to stop by one of these places, it was usually in the company of artists, who are notoriously reluctant to spend money. I preferred to go elsewhere, if only to the Stu Club that had been opened by Tonio Sobański. It was located at the corner of Nowy Świat and the Aleje Jerozolimskie, and was regarded as a rather esthetic establishment, much like Tonio himself. In the afternoons I would go there for tripe soup or *bigos,* a cup of red *barszcz* with a pastry, and black coffee.

He was a rum fellow, that Tonio Sobański! A very characteristic figure, I think, for Warsaw of the time, and the gradual revolution that was taking place in Poland. A count and owner of the magnificent Guzów, he was a Bohemian; he didn't like the country, broke with tradition, and soaked up all the artistic and intellectual ferment of the age. He was in effect disinherited, the black sheep of the family even, and he infuriated his assorted aunts with his blasphemies.

Exceptionally intelligent, a European, a man of great refinement and excellent manners, and a character who attracted the attention of others. He had no special talent of his own, or perhaps could not mobilize it in himself because of an excess of criticism—he agonized over this secretly, found an outlet in company, and was always witty and charming. Charming? Tonio's charm may have been his Achilles heel, but there was no doubting that he was an uncommon individual. I once read a memoir, published abroad somewhere, by a certain Englishwoman who had spent a few weeks traveling round Poland. In her recollections her enchantment at Wawel, Kazimierz on the Vistula, and Wieliczka were so intertwined with paeans of praise for the "delightful Polish count" who accompanied her that in the end it wasn't clear whether she had more admiration for Wit Stwosz's altarpiece or for the witticism that Tonio uttered when they visited it.

In such conditions it isn't hard to be mannered, and I'm afraid that he did not entirely succeed in avoiding this. He simply shone too much, was too conscious of the fact that he was delightful, elegant, a *charmeur*. He also had certain habits that irritated me fearfully; for example, there was a time when, if someone told a good joke over dinner, Tonio would get up from his seat and spin around twice with his napkin in his hand, as if laughter had brought him to his feet. He had a number of irksome little tricks of this kind. Another obsession of his was a constant desire to Europeanize Poland, yet not in a profound sense but rather in its most superficial aspects. Tonio, for instance, wished to stir up public opinion against overly vulgar and simplistic advertising; and so in the cinema, when there appeared an unimaginative slogan such as "Eat Wedel chocolates—they're delicious," Tonio would remark deliberately loudly: "Well, that's a stupid advertisement. But at least we now know not to eat Wedel chocolates!" These and other such initiatives of his, some of which appeared in print in *Wiadomości Literackie*, wrongly brought him a reputation as a snob and an esthete. For this he was most aggressively castigated by the nationalist Skiwski, who, the poor fellow, truly had little in common with estheticism, for his attacks were heavy and loutish, as if he were wielding a plank.

But Tonio was not a snob, nor a mannered elegant. He was, however, a man of the elite, and his field of operations was restricted to the upper spheres. Such people are also necessary. He was one of the most enlightened members of the Polish aristocracy, and that too has its significance. Whoever had encountered those famous aunts of Tonio's knew what a huge leap was needed in order to become the disgrace of that noble line. I personally once had to eject just such a countess, for she really overstepped the mark. At the time I was managing my mother's apartment building, which incidentally provided no income whatsoever from the rents, and this lady was negotiating with me about letting an apartment for her son or some other relative. Not knowing me, and not having properly heard my last name, she imagined that she was dealing with an ordinary manager, of the kind who do not belong to "society"; and in this spirit she began to talk so arrogantly to me that I lost my patience and asked her to leave. Amongst the aristocracy, which was already on its last legs—for most of these people no longer had either estates or positions—such superiority complexes could still sometimes be found, though they didn't usually go unpunished.

In my view Tonio played an extremely important role in the artistic circles of Warsaw, because he represented elegance, taste, distinction, and other similar virtues that were regarded amongst us as "superficial" or even "unmanly," and in any case insufficiently heroic and vigorous. It never seemed to occur to the proponents of vigor such as Skiwski or Piasecki that those sickly and delicate French or Italians were in fact incomparably more resistant to the blows of history than we are, even though we scorn the trills of southern operas and instead adore military marches. Tonio sensed perfectly that the charm of our nation, its ability to fascinate and seduce, could be a weapon no less powerful than a cannon, and that the world has an entirely different attitude toward a nation which impresses with its style, its form, its allure. Spending a great deal of time abroad, he constantly had the opportunity to compare the beauty of Poland—let us call it that, of course in the broader sense of the word—with the beauty of other European and even American nations.

And he would return from these confrontations dispirited. I sometimes happened to hear those moans and complaints, before his impressions, brought back from England, Italy, or the United States, melted away in the drabness of Poland. He was all the more embittered because he saw in us first-rate material, and he believed that the Poles, filled with temperament and imagination and sensitivity to art, could have conquered the world if only they'd not been most dreadfully "stiffened" by a terrible combination of sclerosis, provinciality, prudery, pathos, and a strained, military "manliness."

"How awful they are!" he exclaimed suddenly when we were walking down Nowy Świat one day.

"What's that?" I asked.

"The faces," he replied.

*

In those dance clubs of Warsaw I met Zbyszek Uniłowski. It came about after I'd already published my first book and was working on my next one, *Ferdydurke*. At the time Uniłowski was a lot better known than I was, since *Wiadomości Literackie* had trumpeted him as a candidate for the role of greatest up-and-coming Polish writer, and his novel *A Shared Room* had acquired no ordinary admirer—Piłsudski himself.

One evening I went to the Adria with some people who had nothing in common with literature. We were drinking, chatting, and observing the dancers, when a young and already very rotund young man came up to me and said:

"Mr. Gombrowicz, why are you sitting with these people? Come and join my table!"

I didn't know what to think and looked at my companions to see if they were offended; but they all knew Uniłowski. There was laughter, and I spent the rest of the evening one on one with Uniłowski in literary conversation.

Oh, those conversations with Uniłowski! For there was not just the one. This Uniłowski was already a someone, "the editor" as the waiters called him, a well-known writer, husband of one of the Lilpop daughters, who were popular in Warsaw—she had brought him a beautiful apartment on the Aleja Róż—and he was a wealthy man. He knew that he had money, and he spent it on drink in various establishments, handing out generous tips. These "establishments" may have been an obsession of his, a complex from the time that he himself had waited tables with a napkin over his arm. And so his friendship with me expressed itself above all in his dragging me out to various late-night establishments.

I too immediately took a real liking to him, and I also held him in high esteem as a writer. But despite this we were a thoroughly ill-matched pair, chalk and cheese, and we had little to say to one another. Uniłowski was a member of the proletariat who had achieved social advancement through his talent and intelligence. Like Worcell, he had been a waiter, or even a kitchen boy in some big restaurant, when Karol Szymanowski had discovered him. Szymanowski took him under his wing and helped him to publish his first book, which, if I'm not mistaken, was in fact *A Shared Room*. From that moment this still young lad entered into entirely different circles, where it was far from easy for someone who had to learn from scratch the necessary ways of conversing, the forms and the subtleties. I admired him; I admired how he managed to deal with so many traps and difficulties; but despite all this, he and I couldn't find a common language. And this was more due to our different natures than to culture or upbringing.

I was a man of the cafés; I loved to spout nonsense for hours on end over black coffee and to indulge in various kinds of psychological games. He needed alcohol, dimmed lights, jazz, obliging waiters—at such times he felt that he had succeeded, that he had made it, that he had climbed to the highest floor. Maybe it wasn't so simple; maybe there were many complex reasons that drew Uniłowski to bars and dance clubs; but I think that at least one reason was so he could be a client and a guest in the places where he used to serve.

Was it Uniłowski who told me that the mental exertions of a waiter, who has to remember orders from five tables and not make a mistake, at the same time hurrying about with bowls, bottles, juices, sauces, and salads, are infinitely greater than the exertions of an author trying to arrange the different subtle threads of his plots? "A restaurant, a large restaurant, is less exhausting physically than mentally," he used to say. "You can't get to sleep afterward; for hours into the night, all those 'one tripe soup' and 'roast with mushrooms' keep coming back to you."

He put me in mind of Jack London. There was something kindred in their view of the world, their style, and their intelligence. Uniłowski made up for the gaps in his education and his reading with his realism, directness, temperament, and humor; there was something American about him, and I often used to think that Chicago would have been a more appropriate place for him than Warsaw. But despite my admiration, I couldn't help the fact that our temperaments did not rhyme—we were a rather curious pair of friends, because we liked each other through our books, and we strained to bring our personal relationship up to the level of this higher literary affection. And yet with Adolf Rudnicki, who had similar shortcomings to Uniłowski, I found it infinitely easier to converse and even debate, since Adolf was expansive, lyrical, exceedingly communicative with everyone. Zbyszek Uniłowski was difficult, reserved, highly sensitive, and in a constant state of tension. In addition he was a rebel—like some precursor of Hłasko, perhaps not so much in what he wrote as what he was going to write.

I trusted his intelligence and taste to such an extent that, even though so much divided us, I gave him *Ferdydurke* to read when it was still in typescript. He telephoned me a few days later. "I was mad when I read it," he said. "This is exactly what I wanted to write next. You stole my book."

I believe he was being sincere. He'd already mentioned that he was thinking about writing a satirical work "à la Voltaire," which would be his protest against the world and his settling of accounts with it. He was bubbling with resentment and anger; he wished for vengeance and conflict. *Ferdydurke* was a combative book, and it was probably thanks to this that in Zbyszek I immediately won a far from average reader.

But he continued not to understand me as a person. Because I was not a Bohemian like him, he saw me as an incorrigible, small-minded bourgeois—a bourgeois who by a strange quirk of fate happened to be a poet to whom strange things happened, as they did to Dickens's Pickwick. "Pickwick, Pickwick," he would call out when he saw me, pleased that he had defined me; and yet I wasn't like that. Many things remained unsaid between us; in fact, we never once really had a frank talk. And, what was worse, I didn't fit the style of his jokes, nor he that of mine.

I'm very much afraid that I was the indirect cause of his death.

I had a slight influenza; I was staying home and getting bored. I telephoned him to invite him to supper. He came and caught the influenza, which turned into meningitis. He died.

Perhaps it wasn't from me that he was infected; perhaps the meningitis was caused by something else. But I cannot shake off the suspicion that if he hadn't visited me then, he would still be alive.

The funeral was rich in—let it be said—amusing moments. A huge crowd had gathered in the church at the Powązki Cemetery, since the death of such an exceptionally promising writer had stirred public opinion. *Wiadomości Literackie* had even published a special issue in his honor. But these friends of Zbyszek were for the most part atheists like him—from the ministers and the generals to the most outrageous Bohemians. There were even some who had completely forgotten what the inside of a church looked like, and how to behave during the service.

And so, when the rather embarrassed priest set about celebrating the mass, half the church didn't know when to kneel and when to stand, and in the end it was a small group of the initiated who, with deliberately ostentatious movements, showed the unbelievers what to do.

It was a great pity that he died.

Yes, he had talent—and he was a bold, sharp-witted, gifted, even wise man, though he may still have been far from overcoming his own huge problems. I held him in high regard, though I could never agree with those who considered him a great writer, along the lines of a "Polish Balzac." Oh, those Polish Balzacs, Dickenses, and Prousts! We don't need Polish Balzacs, but the kind of writer who would be quite unlike anyone else, whose writing would be unique, individual, and irreplaceable, of whom it would be said in France: "Oh, that writer of ours, he's a French Uniłowski!" But realism of Uniłowski's kind is too little for today. His literature was neither creative enough nor modern enough to become truly significant.

*

Yet from my perspective today I can see that the whole twenty-year period from 1919 to 1939 was nevertheless a huge leap forward. And perhaps most of all in lifestyle. It was a leap from the little master, dressed in bowler hat, spats, and patent leather shoes and carrying a cane, to the unbuttoned young folk who would enter the Second World War.

The most striking transformation was in conceptions of honor. The catastrophic demise of the old, formal notion of honor, with duels, seconds, and protocols, manifested itself clearly in my immediate family. My father was a gentleman in the old style, from before the first war, and he attached great significance to every kind of correctness; but even he began to show a certain sense of humor regarding the "affairs of honor" that were popular at the time. Once in Małoszyce my mother caught him engaging in a bizarre sport: He was firing a pistol at a figure chalked in profile on a board, and he was obviously aiming at its backside. My mother, who was mightily intrigued, eventually drew out of him that he had been called out to fight a duel and had decided to put a bullet in his opponent's rear end, which happened to be rather sizable.

My older brother Janusz was, I think, more interested in his honor as a merchant than as a member of the gentry; finances played a much greater role in his worldview than the traditions and obligations of caste. He was most amused when Stefan Kozłowski, the husband of one of our cousins, happened to have a rather curious affair of honor: One day, in the restaurant of the Hotel Bristol he noticed that a man sitting nearby was evidently making faces at him. He immediately went up to the fellow and demanded an apology, upon which the other man said that he wouldn't dream of it, that he resented the implication, and so on and so forth. Before it came out that the faces the man had been pulling were not at all directed at Kozłowski but at someone sitting behind him, both men had succeeded in suitably offending one another, and the whole thing ended with a duel, which, however, was luckily bloodless.

On the other hand Jerzy, my other brother, also older than I, during his student days had shown a great fondness for this whole ritual and all the various protocols "in the affair of honor of X, Esq., with Y, Esq."; I suspect, however, that he too was not serious about it. It was a splendid entertainment, abounding in grandiloquent formulas, and the way the two wretched "parties" each "got the wind up" gave it the appearance of genuine danger. These games were indulged in by a large number of students, who had the appropriate specialized knowledge and were thoroughly familiar with Boziewicz's code of honor, thanks to which no dispute could take place without their involvement as seconds, arbiters, or experts. Jerzy relished his participation in these sports, writing impressive protocols in round hand, but he never, as the expression goes, played an active part. I believe that to a certain extent this took the place of today's cinema in providing thrills . . . and soon, as he grew older, this mania of his passed.

And finally me, the youngest. I was utterly "dishonorable" in the sense of Boziewicz's code; in such matters I was a savage, a barbarian, and a simpleton incapable of comprehending the hierarchy of parts of the body and unable to grasp why, for instance, a blow to the face is something more outrageous than a blow to the ear. My morality not only had nothing in common with Boziewicz, it was actually the reverse: For me, the morality of a class, group, or sphere was in fact immorality, and I demanded one law for all. But it wasn't at once that I freed myself from the code of honor. When I was at school, our unwritten schoolboys' code proclaimed that a person slapped was dishonored if he didn't return the slap. This was a much simpler procedure than the complex protocols and formal exchange of bows and shots during a duel, but it also brought complications, because the one whose face was slapped in return was in no way inclined to accept it but at any cost would try to strike back once again. The net result was an endless series of slaps—smack, smack, smack—one after another, often at machine-gun speed, since in their dogged efforts to strike the other's face both opponents left their own unprotected.

Sometimes this honorable pummeling dragged on for months, since the one who had been slapped would not retaliate immediately but instead would wait for an opportunity and only the next day, or a few days later, coming upon his opponent immobilized while eating a roll or putting on his overcoat, would deal him a blow in the so-called "puss."

We also had a special court of honor attached to the student council, but I don't think anyone ever appealed to it. Except for me, once. It happened like this: The president of the council was Grabiński, a serious and responsible young fellow, whose seriousness irritated me and my unruly pals. One day we burst into a sitting of the council and set about causing such a commotion that the furious president in most unambiguous language threw me out. That was all I needed. Of course I took this as an insult and brought the case before the court of honor. The matter dragged on for a fearfully long time and gave us the opportunity to cook up some magnificent documents, till in the end the vacation came, and during the vacation the whole thing evaporated.

It wasn't only amongst schoolchildren that these affairs of honor took on ever more grotesque contours. It was one of those forms that were degenerating before my eyes, though there were others too.

I'm not sure, but I believe that a critical turning point in matters of honor was the war with the Bolsheviks in 1920. I have the impression that this upheaval finally put an end to the age of visiting cards and frock coats; we needed a war, our own war, and a great peril, for the shots of cannon and rifles to silence the popping of pistols. True, there was no shortage of duels in subsequent years—but it was partly out of inertia, and partly a sport for amateurs. Society had become so variegated, so many groups had appeared with different moralities and manners, that someone accused of being dishonorable in one circle could move to another in which it was of no interest to anyone. And in the last instance one could give public expression to one's scorn for "mistaken notions at odds with the spirit of the times" (the press were always glad to print such declarations), and then one passed for a pioneer and a martyr to the cause of true democracy.

Słonimski's jokes at the expense of "honor," for example (in his dedications he would sign himself "child in matters of honor, poet in matters of money, and scribbler—always"), were received with amusement, especially by young people.

Yet sometimes I wondered if this discontinuation of personal responsibility with weapon in hand was in fact not at all democratic—quite the opposite, it constituted yet another privilege of the upper classes. In previous times a man of the gentry lived an advantaged life, but once in a while he was obliged to risk his neck—if not in war, then in a duel. When universal military service made everyone equal as far as wartime was concerned, there still remained the duel as a special risk peculiar to the upper classes and compensating if only in part for all the comforts and privileges that money provides. Yet when this too disappeared, and the portly bourgeois no longer had even this obligation—to exchange shots when he was struck in the face—what did this mean if not total undisturbed sybaritism?

And, interestingly, the softness of our youth was noticed by visitors to Poland; two or three times I heard comments to this effect, and once a certain young German of Polish descent who had transferred from Berlin University to Warsaw University spoke to me almost indignantly of the "mildness" of Polish students, and even their "docility." This surprised me mightily, for it was at a time of nationalist excesses and anti-Semitic violence. But later still I was even more taken aback when I saw how this "mildness" conducted itself so heroically at the front and in the resistance movement.

*

How little I knew Poland! I'm one of those people who like to stay in one place; traveling doesn't excite me. If I left Warsaw it was to go to the country, to Małoszyce near Sandomierz or to stay with one of my brothers, one by Iłżec, the other in the Radom region; or to the mountains or the seaside; or, less frequently, to go abroad. Being neither a hunter nor a cardplayer, I didn't hang around manor houses, nor did business interests oblige me to take trips to the provinces.

Kraków, I'm embarrassed to admit, I visited for the first time when I was nearing thirty, with the almost complete typescript of *Ferdydurke* in my suitcase.

I was on my way to Czorsztyn at the time, and I decided to stop in Kraków to stand face to face with Wawel and with the Polish past in general. It was a vague need that may in part have been motivated by the disquiet that was spreading throughout Europe in connection with the rearming of Germany: I wanted to take a look at that heart of the Polish nation and to check my own reactions. But, I repeat, it was neither a clear nor an urgent matter, and if Kraków had not been en route to Czorsztyn I wouldn't have undertaken this pilgrimage.

Pilgrimage? My feelings were not especially those of a pilgrim; rather the opposite. Not long ago, reading the young Żeromski's account of his trip to Kraków recorded in his journal, I couldn't help juxtaposing his pilgrimage with mine, separated as they were by upward of four decades. Żeromski really was a pilgrim. "With adoration, with trembling hands you touch the marbles and whisper in the depths of your soul: 'O, you most great ones!'" In these words he describes his visit to Wawel, in what he calls "one of life's magnificent moments, like the moment of first communion." As for me, I went there not to genuflect and prostrate myself but to check on myself! Check what, you may ask? I myself wasn't entirely clear. But in any case that excursion had a quality of calculated inspection rather than humble worship.

I arrived at night, booked into a hotel, and the next morning set off for Wawel after taking a look at the market square and vicinity. It was hard not to acknowledge the noble beauty of the city, but something held me back from admiring it—perhaps because this veneration came with such alacrity from other Poles. I preferred to act more cautiously. In the end I walked up Wawel Hill. In front of me there was a party of schoolchildren; the sun was shining; it was a lovely June day. I studied the towers and the walls, the Renaissance and Baroque of the towers and walls, and tried to figure out whether we are closer to the Renaissance or to the Baroque, after which I went inside and began the eternal passage from room to room common to every museum and castle in the world.

In the "Room of the Heads" I heard someone speaking poor French. It was a gentleman trying to explain to two Frenchmen the origins of the tapestries, but not having much success; he was stammering and rolling his eyes in desperation. At several points I provided a word he needed, and we struck up a conversation. It turned out that these were not Frenchmen but Belgians, industrialists who were visiting some nearby factory; he was in the management at this factory and had been assigned to act as guide to the guests because of his knowledge of French. He was bathed in perspiration and asked if I couldn't help him out—he'd prepared well and had a lot to convey, and it was only a question of translating what he would say from the Polish. I agreed, not realizing what I was letting myself in for.

"Please tell them: This is the famous 'Room of the Heads' in which the kings of Poland received envoys from around the whole world. And this is the most magnificent tapestry in the whole collection, a great masterpiece; it is unparalleled in all the world."

I translated, but something displeased him.

"Why did you say that it was a 'beautiful tapestry,' and not a 'master-piece'? What are they saying?"

"They're asking if these tapestries aren't Belgian?"

"Tell them that there was no Belgium at that time! And now, please say that this painting by an anonymous artist of the Flemish school is of extraordinary value and could appear in the best European museums."

I translated again. But my countryman was even less satisfied with me. He eventually asked, "What's the laughter about?"

"We were joking because the ceiling reminds them of a switchboard."

"You know what, sir, thanks for your help, but to be frank I can see you're not serious enough about . . . This can't be! I'd rather just try and communicate with them on my own!"

I didn't need to be told twice. I completed my tour alone, though, alas, in a mood of rising vexation that prevented any more exalted feelings. Yes, Wawel was a jewel, it was true; it's just that sometimes jewelry is a mark of poverty. When your neighbors religiously show you the signet ring of their great-grandfather, you can assume that in the present day the family has gone to the dogs, since they're so impressed by the past. That whole Polish reverence for Wawel more or less worked when we were alone—that is, when no outsiders were present; but when the external world entered the picture, everything immediately became embarrassing, even comic.

And also . . . after all, there in Wawel, in Kraków, one continually came across the names of Italians who had built the place, painted it, sculpted it—this entire splendor was, as if out of spite, a testimony to the fact that at that time our fine arts had been in their infancy. What were we supposed to be proud of? The fact that it was our kings who brought these artists from abroad?

I went into the cathedral. Was I to follow Żeromski and fall on my knees exclaiming, "O, you most great ones!"? For the time which had passed since that romanticism was harsh and difficult. I could no longer permit myself any facile exaltations; my times required me to be critical, austere, and sober. Everything depended on the yardstick by which I would judge those sarcophagi: a local, Polish measure or a European or worldwide one? On our domestic scale they were indeed the highest; but on a universal scale this cathedral was one of many, and these rulers, kings, and poets, some amongst many. Then was I to forget about the world here and enclose myself in my Polishness? Or was it precisely here that my duty was to become a Pole on a world scale, one that is conscious of the presence of the world?

This dilemma appeared to me with extreme clarity at the time, and I realized that it had great significance for me.

But I was still too young and wasn't yet capable of transferring those feelings onto paper—it may have been that my attitude to Poland was not yet properly formed. In any case, I could neither write nor speak of this with any gravity, and the repugnance I felt for the classic Polish adoration found its outlet in mostly rather unsophisticated mockery and provocations.

And so, when I described that visit of mine to Wawel in an article in *Kurier Poranny,* it contained nothing more substantial than jokes, for which I was soundly taken to task by the nationalist Piasecki in *Prosto z mostu.* Truth be told, those little witticisms of mine didn't even deserve that much, since I hadn't written anything so terrible.

Who knows if I did not instinctively choose not to bring these matters to some resolution and some form within myself—what good would it have done? In those years it wasn't possible to speak openly on this subject—bah, a person scarcely dared to *think* openly in that Europe which seemed close to madness, in that artificial, convulsive Poland caught between communism and nationalism. Was the word *nation* not taboo? Everything had to find its outlet first. It was necessary to wait.

*

August 30, 1961

All in all I spent a good few winter months in Zakopane. Neither my work as a court intern, nor my later literary occupations, stood in the way, and my health required it. I usually stayed at the Wojcie-chów, a guesthouse run by Miss Halina Szober, sister of the professor. It was a modest but agreeably situated place on a precipitous hill that became dangerous in times of ice; it was distinguished by copious and tasty meals.

I was supposed to lie on the veranda, in a fur wrap, staring for hours on end at the inevitable Giewont and its environs. The monotony of this activity was broken up by various attractions that changed from season to season. For two seasons the big attraction were the "squelchees," a group of thoroughly unsuspecting young ladies between fifteen and eighteen years of age, nieces of Miss Szober's from somewhere in the provinces, whom we squelched—me and my guesthouse confidant and fellow conspirator Andrzej Koźniewski. "Hey, how about squelching Miss Jolanta a little?" I would suggest to Koźniewski, to which he would reply, "Sure, let's squelch Miss Jolanta some," upon which we would set about squelching Miss Jolanta, who, afraid that her aunt would hear her, restricted herself to a quiet cry that turned into a terrifying suppressed squeal. Naturally there was nothing improper about this squelching—it was just parlor teasing.

We also devised a special code that was comprehensible only to us and our victims. For example, if I asked, "Miss Jolanta, why are you so crepuscular today?", this meant that we would soon set about tormenting Miss Jolanta in a particularly refined manner.

Another attraction were the young Handelsmans, the children of Professor Handelsman. I used to flirt with Anda Handelsman and wrote a little verse in her honor: "The Andes mountains rise up high / But Anda's the one to make me sigh!"

The tedium of sitting in a deck chair gave us an appetite for intense experiences and sometimes led to dramatic tensions—for instance, when a group of learned professors from the Jagiellonian University arrived from Kraków. At this point our carefree meals, taken at a shared table, were transformed into a kind of ceremony whose ponderous pedantry irked me beyond words. The professors would sit at the head of the table and conduct learned conversations to which the other guests would listen reverently. It sometimes happened that one of the professors would lead the discourse and take the floor. I was never fond of professors, and those discussions on philology or history seemed as heavy as a hippopotamus and not much more intelligent. So I behaved rebelliously; at the most solemn moments I would interrupt with a polite, "Would you care for a cake?" or to ask for the salt. Once, when we were regaled with a particularly heavy and unpalatable dish, flour dumplings in some kind of sauce, I protested rather loudly, saying that dumplings for the stomach and dumplings for the mind was decidedly too much. It was hardly surprising, then, that in the end there was a scene and one of the scholars almost threw a chair at me.

Such were the fun and games I had. In later years I behaved more seriously. It's odd that despite all the time I spent there I never properly felt at home in Zakopane, perhaps because I was never a regular patron at Trzaska's or any other restaurant.

As far as writers and artists are concerned, Witkacy was the only one I saw with any frequency—not because I sought out his company, but because I was friends with his close friend Mrs. Wądońska, an intelligent and artistically sensitive person who due to ill health was obliged to live permanently in the mountains. On her part considerable diplomacy was required to maintain some kind of harmony between natures as incompatible as Witkacy's and mine. Though I also often had to admire the great forbearance of the master! For, knowing his difficult character, aggressive egotism, and wearisome eccentricities, I was prepared to break off relations with him at any moment; furthermore, not only did I refuse to play along with him, but in order to stand out even more than I did in other circumstances, I would become a country squire and even a snob. Those conversations of ours truly were bizarre! As Witkacy was, in his own demonic way, relishing the utter stupidity of Mr. X, I would ask: "Is he related to the Platers?" He would break off, turn his lackluster gaze on me, and reply slowly, "I don't know if he's related to the Platers." At this point Mrs. Wądońska would step in hurriedly, waving the wand of peace.

If Witkacy didn't do away with me at once, relegating me to the bottom of his list of friends, it may have been because she told him I wasn't always so foolish. Besides, he himself must have realized that I was responding to his pose with a pose of my own.

Things were worse in larger gatherings or on walks, where he would appear in the company of his court, composed of various abject literary mongrels (since he always sought out those inferior to himself, so he could be their leader and they could worship him). In the rather narrow minds of these admirers there was no room for a pose like mine. If I'd turned into a cocaine addict and a hashish smoker, a phenomenologist and Husserlian, a blasphemer, the devil himself, they would not have been shocked in the slightest; but at the sight of a crass bumpkin like me the ground gave way beneath their feet. They regarded me as an uncommon idiot, an opinion that was entirely mutual.

Despite all this, the sight of that powerful figure striding through the snow on a starry night in the mountains, with his entourage of rapt, adoring halfwits, was most dramatic. One had the impression that some excellent thing had become distorted, thrust beneath a painful buffoonery; it was never so glaringly obvious to me that in Poland the superior and the inferior are incapable of coexistence, but only steep one another in farce. In France I saw people talking to one another like two equals, despite the fact that one of them had three university degrees and a famous name, while the other could barely read or write. Despite their differences they managed to find grounds where they could communicate freely. I've even seen people who were capable of speaking freely about someone else's greatness; in such cases their ease of expression did not diminish their respect.

As I mentioned, other than Witkacy I had few contacts with the artistic circles of Zakopane, which was closely connected with the fact that I rarely visited Krupówka. But once in a while I had an artistic drinking bout. One in particular has stuck in my memory, involving Witold Małcużyński and Colette Gaveau, his present wife and at that time his fiancée. It was after a concert; even in those days Małcużyński liked to have a bit of a drink after a concert to relax. It may even have been that at that time he needed it more, because he was more afraid of the audience.

He poured vodka into himself until in the end he turned white as a sheet and staggered off to the bathroom.

"Witek," Colette exclaimed, aghast, and a moment later ran off after him. And I went too, since I was filled with foreboding.

I was not mistaken. Without a second thought, Colette had followed Małcużyński into the gentlemen's bathroom, which was full at that hour. It isn't hard to imagine the consternation that ensued. The appearance of a tigress could not have caused such a stampede; everyone fled, buttoning up whatever they had to button up.

Oh, and one more drunken recollection. I went to visit an acquaintance of mine and we played chess.

"There's some vodka in the cupboard there," he said. "Let's have a drink."

He drank a glass.

And he died. Such things also happened. Sport and leisure were undermined by the demise of various stiffs.

*

Still on the subject of Zakopane.

Jazz music is blaring, "He's marching on, / The Spanish Don, / The conquering Don Fernando!"

Dawn. The couples refuse to stop dancing even though the music has fallen silent—so the music starts up again da capo! Those are my recollections, the last probably, from Trzaska's and the Morskie Oko restaurant. At last it's over; the jazz musicians are putting away their instruments, people are gathering near the exit, putting on their coats and overshoes, when something comes over them once again; they start spinning around, the music is blasting, overcoats and shawls fly on the whirling clientele. The kind of party that I've seen break out sometimes in the early morning in the clubs of Zakopane, I've never come across anywhere else. Though it's true that I'm no expert on parties.

Yet, hanging about here and there, mostly on the sidelines, in the role of onlooker whom few people knew, I couldn't help observing a process that took place before my eyes during those years in Zakopane. I would describe it as a gradual dying out of circles and styles.

In Zakopane one encountered all kinds of people, which of course in itself would hardly be unusual, since it happens on every street of every city. But these were people at ease, unconcerned with ranks and hierarchies. Country squires from the eastern provinces or from the west, speculators, aristocrats of the Radziwiłł family, professional mountain climbers, Boy-Żeleński and Makuszyński, industry and commerce, the intelligentsia, students, consumptives, highlanders—all mingled together on Krupówki. When I first visited Zakopane around 1927, each of these groups went their own way and had their own language, their own customs, and their own table at Trzaska's. Despite the apparent ease of manners, it was rather hard to move from one group to another; in this regard there were even devilish little tragedies that were no one's fault. For example, what happened to Mr. Y. This Mr. Y accidentally took a room in the wrong guesthouse, and that was his downfall.

I believe it was in 1928, in the Mirabella Guesthouse, owned by one of the Szczuka daughters—I forget whether it was the canoness or her sister. In any case, all the persons who stayed there were recruited from amongst their friends and acquaintances and were, as our grandparents would have said, people "of the right tone," from aristocratic circles. But one morning there arrived in this repository of good breeding a certain gentleman with a thoroughly unfamiliar last name, a young man with magnificent new pigskin suitcases and a dazzling walking outfit. Questions were asked—who is this fellow? No one knew.

Eventually it transpired that he had gotten lost and had pulled up here mistakenly instead of at another guesthouse. But since there happened to be a vacancy, he had been given a room. Dear Lord! This wretched fellow, who after several years of working his fingers to the bone had amassed a little money and had come to Zakopane to give himself a well-earned vacation, the first of his life, had no inkling of the terrible torments to which he had exposed himself. He appeared at dinner in an immaculate pair of knickerbockers, introduced himself to everyone enthusiastically, and, since he was talkative, wished to take part in the conversation.

At this point something dreadful happened. The conversation rejected him. It's hard to put this any other way, since it was no one's fault; quite the opposite, everyone tried to be nice to him, and it never even occurred to anyone to put on airs. It was just that, well, this was a company that had its own topics, its own relatives and acquaintances to talk about, and lastly its own way of joking and making fun. Everyone tried to keep the conversation on neutral ground, but the conversation, like a drunkard, kept staggering into the ditch of its habits, and returning to Staś and the fact that he was marrying

Kasia. But worst of all was that the newcomer couldn't cope in this situation. The usual reaction of a person hearing about things that are of no consequence to him is to become bored or indifferent. But this man was entranced by the very fact that he didn't understand. Such a fascination with others' secrets, the secrets of other circles, was common in those days; Proust describes it in his volume *Within a Budding Grove*. From this moment our Mr. Y lived only from the hope that in the end he would break the ice and would be admitted; and naturally things ended tragically, like any desperate efforts of this kind. He began to push in. And so the others began to push him out.

I took an active part in this drama, since in my character as writer and intellectual I was something of a black sheep in this august company and, having made friends with Y, I stirred him up against all the others. And in the end, when the situation had reached an apogee of absurdity and Y had gone completely off his rocker, I explained to him that his clothes and his luggage were too new, and that because of this he was being treated unfavorably, like a parvenu. We spent a whole evening dragging his garments in the dust and scratching his cases with a penknife so they would look used.

Why am I telling this story? Because it depicts the many-languaged nature of Poland back then, and the ridiculous situations that arose between all those different separate little worlds, which at that time seemed as mighty and impregnable as medieval castles. That year of 1928 was still an age in which Boy-Żeleński would be stared at in admiration and awe as he sat eating a buttered roll in a café. What could he be thinking about? Who was that with him? Was it Krzywicka? What were they talking about? No one would have approached that table without properly preparing the ground first, just as no one would have imposed themselves unceremoniously upon a group of bankers or professors. Then, nine years later—what a change! Young ladies barely come of age would sit down uninvited at writers' tables to ask their opinion on what to read; they were so self-confident, certain they would be welcome, and not at all embarrassed by their own ignorance. A young industrialist would not strain excessively to be refined when he conversed with a count, and, horror of horrors, hardly seemed curious about the latter. It was the end of the myth that there existed closed groups with a patent on culture, fashion, or intelligence, or new, deluxe sins of the kind Witkacy used to shock people with. Naivety was disappearing, and with it many splendid kinds of adoration and rapturous fascination. People were more engaged in living their own lives.

If I'm not mistaken (for I sometimes get the exact dates mixed up), eight years passed between my first visit to Mrs. Kasprowicz's on Harenda and the next, which was also the last. The first visit took place in an atmosphere of reverence almost; if any attempt at simplicity was made, it was the kind that accompanies pilgrims, and the whole thing reminded me of a second-rate Wawel—I was fearfully bored on that occasion. The second visit was more like a day trip; we poured out of the automobile in high spirits, and we only remembered about Kasprowicz on the way back. Maybe it was by chance—or perhaps it was the spirit of the times?

At the time, in my soul I was on the side of the evolution breaking down all the cults and the deference that seemed to me simply unwise, as they deprived Poles of their liberty and their boldness. Today, after twenty years in America, where people do not concern themselves with the splendors of others, whether it's a millionaire, a dignitary, an artist, or a great scholar, where a ten-year-old boy will converse as freely with an adult as the adult would converse with Einstein, I sometimes actually feel nostalgia for the old "hindrances," the old blushes and the awkwardness that comes from admiration.

It may have been more interesting. Naturally, it's pleasant to feel confident and at ease with everyone, not to allow oneself to be impressed or to take too much of an interest in anyone else, to devote oneself to one's own business. And yet we've lost something when we cease to sense in the next person some magnificent, unattainable secret, and when there are no longer tensions between different social circles. Does anyone impress anyone else in today's Poland? I doubt it. You've acquired some wisdom, then; but you may have lost some poetry.

*

Jews played such a remarkable and characteristic role in the development of Poland in those years that they cannot be passed over. I was attracted to them from my earliest youth. I liked their intellectual vigor, their spiritual unrest, their critical and rational character; and at the same time, on many occasions they provided me with wonderful entertainment, because they were rich in foibles and amusing idiosyncrasies.

It might seem that my origins in the landed gentry would have instilled anti-Semitism in me. Nothing of the sort! In my family at least, anti-Semitism was regarded as a sign of narrow-mindedness, and none of us was ill-disposed toward Jews, though we may have retained certain prejudices of a social nature. And in any case, the anti-Semitism of the gentry was not dangerous: The "destructive role" of the Jews was criticized, but every squire had his Jew, with whom he would sit on the verandah for hours in secret conversations testifying to a coexistence that had lasted for centuries.

One of my cousins, gifted with a sense of humor not infrequently found amongst the gentry, would converse with his Israelite not on the verandah but from a second-floor balcony, so that he could yell down at the merchant standing in front of the house: "What are you trying to tell me, Moishe?!" I imagine that many people would see this as a typical manifestation of the gentry's pompousness; but I think that my cousin, in turning himself into a proud master and the merchant into a poor "Moishe," was making a rather profound joke—for he was mocking himself as much as the Jew, and turning the very attitude of the gentry toward the Jews into something grotesque.

At school I had little contact with Jews, since it was a hyper-Catholic and conservative institution. Those few Jews who attended it were from plutocratic spheres that were attracted to the aristocracy and were marked by intense snobbery. These boys were well dressed; they had money, they played stylish sports like tennis, and they had the sophistication that comes of frequent travels abroad. And yet it was enough to draw close to them, to enter their homes and their families a little, for that whole superficial elegance to start to fall apart, revealing unpleasant and amusing things beneath. I had a few uncles who were married to Jewish women from that same plutocracy, but I rarely saw them; as I recall, at first glance those aunts of mine looked nice, even distinguished.

It was only at university that I had more contact with Jewish circles, and I immediately discovered their otherness, within which I could move much more freely, since it contained something extravagant that eluded control. From that moment my friendship with Jews began to blossom, and in the end in the Ziemiańska Café I became known as "the King of the Jews," since it was enough for me to sit down at a table to be surrounded by hordes of Semites; at the time they were my most gracious listeners. But was it only unconstraint and intellectual courage that attracted me to the Jews, or did that fondness of mine not have a more specific basis? It was only a long time later, after I had written several books, that I realized—as I did only in the last years before the war—that I happened to have one thing in common with them: my attitude to form.

The Jews are a tragic nation that over the course of centuries of banishment and oppression has been subject to many distortions. It's no surprise, then, that the form of a Jew, his manner and his way of speaking, sometimes has a flavor of the grotesque. The ghetto Jews with their beards and gaberdines, the ecstatic poets from the artists' cafés, the millionaires at the stock exchange: Almost all of them were in one way or another grotesque, almost implausible as a phenomenon. And as Jews are intelligent, they sense it—they sense it but are unable to free themselves from this bad form. And it's because of this that they often feel themselves to be a caricature, an eccentric joke of the Creator. This tension in the Jew's relation to form; the fact that it torments him so, or renders him laughable, or humiliates him; the fact that a Jew is never fully himself in the way that a peasant or a squire is himself, thoroughly comfortable in a form he has inherited from preceding generations; the fact that a Jew always has to be some compromise of form and its catastrophe; all this made the Jews fascinating to me. For that was what I was striving for in my art—to bring out people's struggles with form, so they should comprehend its tyranny and fight against its violence.

These were matters that were virtually impossible to understand for those of my circles, who moved, spoke, thought, and felt in ways that had been established once and for all and had been inherited from their forefathers. It was only when war and revolution shattered this ritual and began to knead people like wax dolls, and when everything which had seemed eternal turned out to be frail and transitory, that these ideas of mine gained strength. But by then I had already observed, precisely in relation to the Jews, how frequently the proud, seigneurial ways of the people of my sphere broke down in a truly pathetic manner. The Jews seemed an embarrassment with respect to whom it was not possible to behave properly.

How often was I witness to such lamentable, painful embarrassments! The gentry and the aristocracy intermarried with the Jews in order to feather their nests, but they never ceased to be ashamed of these connections, and the unfortunate creatures born of these alliances were never fully accepted in the salons. People quite simply pretended that they knew nothing; good manners dictated that in the company of such a creature one should avoid any mention of the Jews. One never spoke of them, just as one never speaks of the gallows in the house of a hanged man. Krysia Skarbek, a lovely young lady whose heroic role in the war is well known, and who died tragically a few years ago in London, belonged to this very category of the results of mixed marriages. Her father was a count and her mother a Goldfeder. In her presence Jewish topics were shunned, and she herself, the poor thing, never brought it up, and for the longest time everything was fine; till one day there came disaster. It happened in front of the Hotel Bristol, I believe, in Zakopane.

She was staying in the hotel, and at the time she was sitting on a deck chair on the verandah in the company of various titled individuals, when suddenly an older Jewish woman, broad in the beam and rather garishly dressed, stopped in front of the hotel. Not seeing Krysia in her seat on the verandah, she began calling out at the top of her voice, "Krysia, Krysia!" The company was immobilized with fear, most of all the unfortunate Miss Skarbek; instead of answering, she pretended that she didn't hear, that she was not the one being called.

But all to no avail, since the cry resumed, and this time there could be no doubt: "Krysia Skarbek! Krysia Skarbek!"

You should have seen this group of people, who after all were experienced in the ways of the world: eyes staring fixedly at the ground, faces drawn. All looked as if they had been suddenly struck down with paralysis. What a blessing it would have been if someone had said simply, "Krysia, don't you hear? One of your aunts is calling you!"

But no one was capable of uttering such simple words. As if turned to stone, they continued valiantly to pretend that they knew nothing about anything, despite the cries sounding ever more loudly. In this there was neither contempt nor hatred—it was merely a fearful helplessness, an inability to overcome convention, to summon up a more modern style.

In such abrupt confrontations there appeared to me the entire ungainliness of these Polish forms passed down unaired from long ago, and their utter inapplicability to life.

I slowly began to perceive that this Jewish world grafted onto the Polish world had an extremely subversive effect—and that this represented one of our best opportunities to devise a new species of Pole with a modern form capable of facing up to the present day. The Jews were what connected us to the most profound and most difficult problems of the world.

When I entered the law department of Warsaw University in the year of Our Lord 1923, the nationalist and anti-Semitic movement amongst young people was far from the sorry extremes it reached just before the war. During the whole of my time at the university I never witnessed any anti-Semitic incidents—though, in truth, I rarely went to the university, preferring to study the assigned readings at home.

From the beginning I became close with a number of my fellow students of Semitic origin, with whom I studied for the exams. This was my first intellectual contact with Jews. I was struck above all by the extent to which these colleagues differed from the Arians when it came to knowledge about the world and about people. My conversations with Arians were placid, and usually I learned nothing from them that I didn't already know myself—to a great extent we had access to the same sources of information in the form of newspapers, books, family discussions, and so on. While from the Jews I learned, for example, about the possibility of a crisis in the United States, the prospects of Trotskyism, the poetry of Przyboś—things that were often utterly exotic, as if these Jews had their own separate press. I would pull a skeptical face and pretend that it was of little interest to me, but in reality I would prick up my ears, sensing that these were far from banal matters.

My Jewish friends took an instant liking to me. I think the secret of my success arose from the fact that I made no concessions to them; quite the opposite even, with my natural contrariness I emphasized all my qualities as an Arian and a member of the landed gentry. You're familiar by now with my strategy. Well then, in my view Jews have a weakness for a fellow from the Polish gentry; he amuses them and makes them laugh, since in his company they feel more like Jews, that is, like themselves, and that allows them to live more colorfully and intensely. And if, as in my case, my game didn't conceal any antipathy or pride, but on the contrary, rather expressed approval, a splendid game began between me and them that revolved around a mutual delectation of the other's distinctness—and since they have a well-developed sense of humor, it wasn't hard for me to see the glint of laughter in their eyes when I would join them. We played at squire and Jew, and through the game we overcame this burning problem better than could have been achieved with pedantic declarations of equality and other such "progressive" arguments of the intelligentsia.

But I only really got to know them when I entered the literary world and took up my nightly post in the artists' cafés of the capital.

At that time it was already apparent that there existed between us a spiritual bond far from superficial in nature. Who supported me, who fought for me on the literary battleground if not them? Who first dared to cast his entire enthusiasm on the scales of the gathering debate over *Ferdydurke* if not my great, sorely missed friend Bruno Schulz? Who cleared a path for me in Poland both before and after the war, if not Artur Sandauer? And in emigration, who supported me more than Józef Wittlin? Always and everywhere, the Jews were the first to sense and to understand my work as a writer. It was so clearly pronounced that I sometimes wondered if a drop of their blood did not flow in my veins; but I'm blond and have a Slavic nose, and I could find no Israelite ancestor on the distaff side of my family tree however far back I searched. Nevertheless—perhaps because on my mother's side I came from a family that abounded in various psychological aberrations—I had in me something of their decadence and their intellect.

Yet my intellectual, even spiritual relations with Jews never once crossed over into personal friendship. Schulz was someone extraordinarily close to me—we spent hours on end discussing matters of art that we felt passionate about—but I felt a hundred times more at home with any old relation of mine from the country. Schulz's private existence was of no interest to me; for me he was a consciousness and a susceptibility *in abstracto.*

Once Lechoń, during one of his visits to Poland—for at that time he was an attaché in the Polish embassy in Paris and lived permanently in France—happened to sit at the adjoining table in the café, and he had the opportunity to overhear one of my dialogues with the Jews who at that time constituted the bulk of my audience.

The next day I met with him, since he wanted to speak with me about *Ferdydurke*. "Yesterday I heard you attacking Jewish naivety," he said.

That made me think. I hardly knew Lechoń, and this may have been my first conversation with him one on one; and so I asked him what he meant.

"You see, I'm very familiar with the Jews," more or less went his reply. "I know them so well I could write a treatise on them. Those who don't know the Jews think that they're cunning, double-dealing, calculating, callous—whereas you have to eat a barrel of herring with them to know that they are naive. The point is, though, that it's a naivety hitched to cunning, and also a romanticism (because they're more romantic than Chopin) hitched to level-headedness; you know, they're naively un-naive and romantically level-headed."

This formula seemed a little too facile for my liking, and I protested, but he interrupted me:

"Listen, when I heard you teasing them yesterday I thought to myself at once: Now there's a fellow who'll teach them a lesson! There's a fellow who's found their Achilles heel!"

I was somewhat suspicious of these compliments of Lechoń's, since I regarded him as a rather insincere character. But I was struck by the accuracy of his observation, as concerned both the general qualities of the Jews and the hidden meaning of my own polemic with them. Yes, it was not their intellectual coldness that bothered me, but precisely the naivety with which they allowed themselves to be impressed by intellect . . . that trusting, almost childlike admiration of scientific reason, theory, doctrine, and ultimately of culture in general. Those dangerous destroyers and revolutionaries were mostly as good-natured as children; you only needed to scratch them to discover dreamers filled with an almost mystic faith—their sharpness mingling curiously with their softness. I've never encountered such dovelike natures as some of those cynics. And I really did tease them as best I could for their naivety. My strategy was to switch roles—so that they should become the romantics, instead of me.

I naturally had much more success at this with novices freshly arrived from the provinces than with people more secure in the capital and in themselves. Writers such as Ważyk or Wat either did not notice me at all or showed no trust in me whatsoever. Their too-dry minds couldn't figure out what to make of someone like me. Ważyk, for example, for several years "would not take me seriously," even though his wife, a painter, was a member of my circle and even painted my portrait. It was only after *Ferdydurke* appeared that Ważyk came up to me and said, "Congratulations, you've broken through!" Yet this acknowledgment remained without any consequences, for Ważyk's intellect, his surrealism, his avantgardeness to me were too redolent of theory and, frankly, Ważyk bored me.

To end, I'll tell you about a dream I had. When did I have this dream? It may have been during the Red Army's offensive against Warsaw, when I was sixteen years old. I dreamed that I was looking out of a second-floor window in our house at Małoszyce. The beautiful garden sloped down toward the pond, beyond which were what was known as the islands, and beyond them . . . [ending missing]

*

After Piłsudski died clear signs of breakdown began to appear. This Poland, less than twenty years old, lacked established principles, institutions, and procedural norms, and all that democracy hadn't yet entered the nation's bloodstream. As long as the panorama of political and even intellectual life was dominated by the strong personality of the Marshal, everything held together rather well—the more so because Piłsudski was far removed from any theory. No one really knew what his principles were, but he inspired confidence as someone who was disinterested yet gifted, brilliant perhaps, perhaps even a savior.

When he died we felt rather as if the wind had torn the roof from over our heads. It was right at a time when things were growing ever more turbulent in Europe. I won't describe the process of disintegration, to which we were not alone in being subjected, but I shall restrict myself to a few personal experiences that I think were typical of the country.

As I recall, it began from astonishment. I think it would be extremely difficult to explain to the new generation just how astonished we were at that time. The tone and the content of what Hitler and Mussolini were introducing into Europe truly seemed quite fantastical. After all, we were utterly convinced that progress meant individual freedom, respect for the law, democracy, demilitarization, pacifism. The League of Nations, and then culture, art, science . . . And here we were hearing about theories that were virtually medieval, and about facts that we regarded as no longer possible in our own century: the reemergence of German militarism, the invasion of Abyssinia, the war in Spain, but above all a thousand small incidents showing that a significant number of Europeans were becoming strangely different, almost exotic.

For us in Poland it was all the stranger because we'd been kept at a distance from the dramatic tensions of Europe, and we were unaware of the pressure exerted by communism. For us Russian communism was something sluggish and rather savage, Asiatic; we were nursed on the belief that the Russian giant still stood on feet of clay. In Poland organized communist activity was almost nonexistent, and we were insufficiently conscious of the powerful threat posed by revolutionary movements in Germany or Italy. We yielded to the illusion that Europe was a sun-drenched meadow, whereas in reality it was a cauldron heated by the fire of revolution and under pressure of a thousand atmospheres.

In our literary circles there soon appeared the first swallows announcing this foreign corruption coming to us from the West. It began, of course, with anti-Semitism—though this anti-Semitism was also somehow inauthentic and fearfully trashy. My table in the Ziemiańska and later in the Zodiak was not a place where particularly fastidious criteria were applied in the selection of company; quite the opposite, I was drawn to inferior kinds of people, eccentric types, scribblers, weirdos, and dubious, unsophisticated creatures from the margins. And so when we were joined one time by Mr. Brochwicz-Kozłowski, a journalist and author of a volume of short stories, I welcomed him with friendly interest, because he was a groveling coward and a hysterical bully consumed by a desire to rise to the top and prey to a sense of his own weakness, arrogant and fainthearted, a slyboots and a ham.

Brochwicz sucked up to me endlessly; he admired me, loved me, adored me, worshipped me, and he did everything he could to win my good graces. But he made up for his obsequiousness toward me by vilifying others of our group, especially those who didn't know how to fight back. I allowed him to do so—up to a point—because it amused me, but in fact I kept him on a short leash.

The growing pollution of the air we breathed nowhere had a more tangible effect than on this Brochwicz. Somewhere around 1936 Brochwicz was a rather low but mostly harmless hysteric. In 1937 a disagreeable grimace appeared in the corners of his mouth, and out of nowhere he began making anti-Semitic remarks to the Jewish women who used to sit with us—Gizella Ważyk, Bela Gelbhadt, or "Gina," a young poet later tortured to death by the Germans.

Naturally I put him sharply in his place once or twice; but to my surprise it didn't help. Gradually we began to feel that something had shifted in the balance of powers. Brochwicz was no longer alone, devoid of friends, and obliged to fawn and seek our approval, and his accomplice was not Polish anti-Semitism, local and rather good-natured. It seemed as if he had found his element, but we didn't properly know why; we hadn't yet experienced that terrible quality of revolutions by which they bring to the surface all manner of human trash, the very dregs of society.

In 1938 Brochwicz became enigmatic and took on an unpleasant tone, supposedly jokingly but with hidden menace. People began to mutter that he was a spy. For whom? The Poles? Some other power? I found it rather hard to believe that he might be working for Hitler, since it turned out that his mother was evidently, visibly Jewish. At that time, in my naivety I imagined that a Jewish mother constituted a certain obstacle on the road to Nazism—the example of Piasecki, the editor of *Prosto z mostu,* a raging anti-Semite whose mother was also Jewish, was not enough for me to understand in my obtuseness that in times of revolution such sordid combinations were the order of the day, and belong to the natural way of things.

In that year, thirty-eight, in April or May I was planning to take myself off to Italy to relax after the exhausting birth of *Ferdydurke.* Brochwicz was also going to Italy and insisted that we set out together. I hesitated, but in the end succumbed—what won't a person do to avoid being alone on the train.

Naturally he'd exhausted me and bored me before we even crossed the Polish border. But it was only the next day that I realized the extent of my madness, as I sat with him in the dining car listening to him slurping his soup with a noise that drowned out the sound of the train and caused a sensation throughout the car.

We stopped for a few days in Vienna, where I lost sight of him, since I had many acquaintances to visit. From Vienna we traveled directly to Italy. At the border in Tarvisio, to my amazement we were not searched at all, and the stationmaster came to Brochwicz with the offer of a private compartment. I was most taken aback, since I doubted that the renown of *Ferdydurke* had reached as far as Tarvisio, while my companion's literary accomplishments were such that in my opinion he deserved a prison cell more than his own compartment. But we were still so naive in those days! In Rome we took up residence in a stylish hotel on the Via Vittorio Veneto. Once again

I was surprised that Brochwicz could afford such a place. As far as I could I avoided sharing my meals with him, since he slurped his spaghetti much as he had his soup; so we rarely saw one another.

All at once I understood. It was in the Vatican, as I was strolling from room to room. Yes, he must be a Nazi agent! I was led to this conclusion not by any facts or logical arguments but only by nuances and tones . . . yes, the tone of his conversation with that German while we were still in the train, as we were leaving Vienna. I remembered the scene. The German was an ardent Nazi; in Brochwicz, because of the nonaggression treaty he saw an ally. They fell into conversation in the corridor of the car, and I listened without understanding much. But now, as I recalled Brochwicz's behavior, his servility, that characteristic fearful eagerness of his, I understood—yes, that was the tone of an agent, a spy!

*

I wish to say some more about that trip to Italy. It was my last encounter with Europe, not counting my glimpses of the coast of France in Boulogne and of England in the fog of the English Channel a year later.

Spring in Italy was magnificent. I warmed myself in the sun in the gardens of the Villa Borghese, a stone's throw from my hotel; I went to the ocean at Ostia, and spent more time wandering about, eating snails and washing them down with Chianti, than fulfilling the duties of a tourist in the museums and churches. That rambling took control of me. The great exertion of *Ferdydurke* was behind me; I felt as if I were on vacation. I had no plans, and even no desire to entertain myself. At that very moment the jury of *Wiadomości Literackie* was deciding the prize for the best book of 1937, and I'd already spent those few thousand zloties in advance—rashly, as it transpired, since the prize was given to Boy-Żeleński for *Marysieńka*. But I cared little about this; I knew that with the prize or without it, I had entered Polish literature for good. I was taking my rest.

Yet at the same time I was horrified.

The buildings of Rome and its paintings—this I knew; it had bored me years before, in Paris. I so hated museums and all that artistic opulence, the excess of which makes one's head ache, that I visited only the Forum. Despite everything, though, that pure, pellucid Latin climate with its ancient aroma, a separate discipline unto itself, swept over me, and I soaked it in through every pore. But in that air and against that noble landscape there was also something turbid and monstrous, a specter as if from a nightmare. The newspapers carried shrill praise of the Berlin-Rome Axis, and the stench of black-mail and betrayal—for me, the conspiracy between Italy and Germany meant the betrayal of Europe—dominated the streets, Mussolini's speeches, the fascists' songs, and even the soldier games played by the brats in front of the Villa Borghese.

I went to a reception given by a certain female singer, whose name I don't recall. Regaled with wine, I listened intently to that bel canto of theirs which is so familiar to the Polish ear. Then suddenly something snapped and politics burst in; the guests grew excited and began waving their arms about and trumpeting the praises of *il Duce!* The aging primadonna suddenly burst into tears, her face in her hands, her pearls dangling, lamenting that her music had been spurned, that no one wanted arias any longer but only politics! That image remains with me; I can see her, crushed, slumping in an armchair.

On the Forum shady individuals approached me offering to be my guide and indicating that they had been persecuted by the police for their political views; this seemed a new method of extracting money from American tourists.

I wasn't able to speak freely with any of my Italian acquaintances (admittedly there were not many of them). And perhaps not because they were afraid, but because they were disoriented. Truth be told, no one knew anything any more. A dreadful doubt—perhaps il Duce is after all the man of the hour and an infallible leader—ate away like a cancer at that always level-headed Latin character. It ate away at the Poles too.

I was buying cigarettes at a kiosk when an individual with ruddy hair, pale blue eyes, and a straight flat nose came up: A Pole! He bought cigarettes and asked in Polish, "Do you have any portraits of Mussolini?"

The question was accompanied by his pointing a finger at a picture of the leader. As he received the portrait he gave a devout sigh: "Oh, we could use a fellow like this in Poland; yes indeed, sir, he's just what we need."

The cigarette seller naturally didn't understand a word, but he was obviously used to comments of this kind from foreigners, and he replied immediately with equal devoutness, "Si, si, il Duce great, Mussolini leader!"

To which my Pole added in rapture, "Mussolini! Mussolini!"

And the cigarette seller ecstatically, "Mussolini! Mussolini!"

These jabberings rather accurately reflected the international situation. I walked away. How difficult it was to make anything out in the mists of those times. Everyone was waiting for a verdict from History, but History was not in any hurry; it was unclear who was lying, who was bluffing, and who was genuine. Contours were blurred and boundaries washed away.

I "made contact," as they say, with the Polish community in Rome and spent one evening with my countrymen. One only, because we didn't take a liking to one another. I noticed immediately that those of them who had been in Rome for a long time considered themselves to be "rather better." They were terribly Latin and Hellenic, and when they encountered a poor savage newly arrived from Poland, they turned up their noses as if they personally had painted all the ceilings at the Quirinal. In order not to disappoint them I accepted the role of barbarian and performed it so well, and uttered so many fearful anticultural heresies, that they paid the bill as quickly as they could and went off home. The next day I boarded a train that was to take me to Venice.

On the way I got to know a group of airmen who were also traveling to Venice, on leave to see their families. We talked all night and, already friends, arranged to meet the following day on St. Mark's Square.

That "salon of Europe" was deserted; I don't know if the season had not yet begun, or if there was a smell of gunpowder because of Austria. The pigeons, and the blue of sky and earth, were infused with melancholy and abandonment.

"Very well, but what if *il Duce* ordered you to bomb all this?" With a sweeping gesture I took in the church, the palace, the Procuratorium.

"Then not one stone would be left on a stone," replied the oldest of them, who was maybe twenty-five, in his broken French. This answer didn't surprise me. It was to be expected. But I *was* surprised at the joy with which he spoke—his eyes shone, and he virtually proclaimed it to me; and on his friends' faces, when they found out what was being said, I also read an unconcealed satisfaction. What were they so pleased about? Was it not that they felt themselves to be creators of history? The past had become less important than the future, and it could be destroyed.

That week in Venice was onerous, poisoned with some savage element that seeped into the calm of the Renaissance and the Gothic.

I was in a somber mood as I returned homeward. It was growing dark, the train was racing toward Vienna, and I had the impression that it was whisking me off into darkness; it was becoming harder to make out shapes, tiny lights appeared in unknown regions, and the rocking of the train as it rushed into that space was turning apocalyptic. And then I suddenly realized that I wasn't the only one afraid.

Around me, in the compartment and in the corridor, everyone was scared. Faces were drawn; some comments were exchanged, remarks were made. What was it? Something had obviously happened. But I was reluctant to ask anyone.

When we drew into the suburbs of Vienna I saw crowds of cheering people with torches. Cries of "Heil Hitler" reached our ears. The city was in a frenzy.

I understood: It was the *Anschluss*. Hitler was entering Vienna.